Thirty Lessons for Those Who Fast

Aa'id Abdullah al Qarni

Copyright ©

King Fahd National Library Cataloging-in-Publication Data

All rights reserved. No part of this book may be reproduced or transmitted in any form or by any means, electronic or mechanical, including photocopying, recording, or by any information storage and retrieval system, without written permission from the Publisher.

Contents

Introduction 7

Guidance of the Prophet in fasting 11

Why was fasting ordained? 16

The Majestic Quran and the month of Ramadan 20

The chants of those who fast 24

Ramadan is a school for the learning of generosity and sacrifice 28

Ramadan: the month of standing up at night 32

The Islamic home in Ramadan 36

How does the heart fast? 41

How does the tongue fast? 46

How does the eye fast? 50

How does the ear fast? 54

How does the stomach fast? 58

Mistakes made by those who fast 64

Our memories in Ramadan 69

Ramadan: the way for repentance 74

Faith increases in Ramadan 78

The love of Allah becomes greater in Ramadan 84

How do we train our children during Ramadan
and at other times? 90

The occurrence of waste during Ramadan 94

Ramadan: the month of righteousness and contact 98

Ramadan: the month of mercy to Muslims 102

How can we revive the traditions in Ramadan? 107

Letter to Muslim woman on the occasion
of Ramadan. 112

Concerns of the Islamic scholar during
month of Ramadan 117

Ramadan calls for the preservation of time 121

Images of love and brotherhood are manifested
in Ramadan 124

Ramadan is a blessed month for the Islamic call 129

The prayer of the fasting person is never refused 134

Gifts to those who fast 139

Tomorrow is Eid – the festival of the breaking
of the fast 142

Conclusion 145

Introduction

Allah

guided us to Islam and exalted us with prayers and fasting. May He bestow His peace and blessings upon His noble prophet, Muhammad, the Imam of all the Messengers, and the best of those who ever pray and fast. We implore similar favour upon his relatives, companions and those who came after them.

I have gathered in this book, *Thirty Lessons for Those who Fast* the most pertinent Quranic verses, authentic *hadith*s, delightful poetry and touching advice. It is, therefore, a book for the righteous when they meet for pleasant conversations. It is also a gift for wayfarers when they break their journeys for rest, a treasure for those who share mutual love and respect, when they assemble for picnics. It is, in addition, an asset for counsellors in their lectures. Indeed, the teacher will benefit from it, the orator will turn to it and the imam of the mosque will find it rewarding to read.

This book is intended to serve three purposes:

First, to document its advice and words which soften the heart with verses from the Glorious Quran and the authentic *hadith*s. It does not contain a single weak *hadith*, bogus story or absurd tradition.

Second, through these lessons I also intended to sow the ers. My aim was not to highlight legal rulings or issues, as we are quite satisfied with the efforts of our eminent scholars who have enriched the Islamic libraries with their writings. Truly, the field of juridical rulings is packed with scholastic contributions. We remain, however, in dire need of works relating to spirituality, basic morals and sublime calls. I trust that this effort will fulfil this demand.

Third, I have taken special care to clothe these lessons in the garments of attractive literature and present them with exquisite expression and eloquence. Toward this end, we embraced the methodology of the Noble Quran and the pure prophetic traditions with their beautiful language so that the reader will find himself between a scrub and rivulet, garden and oasis, water and shade and drizzle and dew.

It was confirmed that when the Prophet Muhammad ﷺ witnessed the new moon at the beginning of Ramadan he would say: 'My Lord and your Lord is Allah, O crescent of goodness and guidance. O my Lord! Let it dawn upon us with peace, submission, security and faith.' Surely Ramadan is the noblest month and its days are the sweetest days. The righteous rebuke Ramadan because of the shortness of its visit and the length of its absence. For it comes after much longing and makes amends after separation. It is often greeted thus:

Welcome to the month of fasting,
O beloved who visits us every year.

We have met you with overflowing love,
All love except for the Holy Master is prohibited.

Accept O my Lord our fast
And increase us from your great favour.

Do not punish us because we were already
punished by sleepless anxiety in darkness.

Strangely enough, Allah mends hearts with the coming of this guest. He forgives sins with his visit, and covers up faults with its arrival.

Welcome to you dear Ramadan!

Lesson 1

Guidance of the Prophet in fasting

All praise is due to Allah. May He bestow His peace and blessings upon His Prophet, his relatives, companions and those who are loyal to him.
Ibn al Qayim mentioned that: 'Among the guidance of the Prophet ﷺ in the month of Ramadan was his engagement in many forms of worship. The angel Gabriel used to teach him the Quran in this month. Whenever Gabriel met him he was more generous than a guided breeze. He was, ordinarily, the most charitable person, and yet when Ramadan arrived he became even more generous. He gave much charity and engaged in kind acts, recitation of the Quran, prayers, remembrance and retreat during this month.'

He used to apportion to Ramadan a degree of worship that was not set aside to any other month. Some times he actually used to continue into the night. The Prophet, however, forbade his companions from doing so. When they pointed out to him that he continued he responded saying: 'My body is not like yours, I dwell with my Lord, He feeds me and gives me drink' (Bukhari and Muslim). Accordingly, Allah Almighty used to nourish His Prophet ﷺ during those periods of extended fasts with subtle knowledge, and abounding wisdom and light of the message. Of course, it was not food and drink in the literal sense, for if this were so the Prophet would not be considered fasting.

When the Prophet ﷺ became satisfied from the worship of his creator, and his heart opened up to his aim, and his mind rested with the remembrance of his Master, and his condition improved by his closeness to His Lord, he forgot all food and drink. As it was said: spiritual power is in the essence of souls, it is not dependent on food or drink. Nothing can harm you, if you have attained the knowledge of your Lord.

The Prophet Muhammad was the best of those who remembered and worshipped Allah. As for the month of Ramadan, it was made to be a season of worship and a time for remembrance and recitation. His nights were spent in supplication and humiliation unto his Lord, seeking His help, support, victory and guidance. He read long chapters of the Quran and stayed for long periods bowing (in *ruku'*) and prostrating himself before Him. Such was the desire that was never satisfied with worship, making his standing in the night a source of sustenance and supply as well as power and energy. Allah Almighty says: 'O Thou enwrapped one! Keep awake [in prayer] at night, all but a small part' (73:1).

يَٰٓأَيُّهَا ٱلْمُزَّمِّلُ

'And rise from thy sleep and pray during part of the night [as well], as a free offering from thee, and thy Sustainer may well raise thee to a glorious station [in the life to come]' (17:79).

وَمِنَ ٱلَّيْلِ فَتَهَجَّدْ بِهِۦ نَافِلَةً لَّكَ عَسَىٰٓ أَن يَبْعَثَكَ رَبُّكَ مَقَامًا مَّحْمُودًا

During the days of the fasting month, the Prophet ﷺ spent his time in propagating the Islamic call, engaging in *jihad*, providing advice and training, and reminding his companions. Among his practices was that the Prophet ﷺ never commenced the fast of Ramadan except with a vision of what was to be achieved. He used to encourage his companions to partake of a meal before daybreak. Indeed, it was confirmed that he said: 'Have the meal before daybreak, because there is blessing in it.' The period before daybreak is considered blessed because it is in the last third of the night, the time of divine descent and forgiveness. Allah says: 'And in the hours of early dawn, they were found praying for forgiveness' (51:18).

وَبِٱلْأَسْحَارِ هُمْ يَسْتَغْفِرُونَ

He also says: 'Those who show patience, firmness and self-control; who are true (in word and deed); who worship devoutly; who spend in the way of Allah; and who pray for forgiveness in the early hours of the morning' (3:17).

ٱلصَّٰبِرِينَ وَٱلصَّٰدِقِينَ وَٱلْقَٰنِتِينَ وَٱلْمُنفِقِينَ وَٱلْمُسْتَغْفِرِينَ بِٱلْأَسْحَارِ

Still besides, the meal before daybreak helps the individual in his fast and worship. It is, therefore, a payment for the bounty of worship that Allah has bestowed upon us.

It was also established that the Prophet ﷺ used to hasten to have a meal after the setting of the sun. He, likewise, ordered his companions to do the same. Usually he had dates or water because something sweet was most agreeable for an empty stomach. Several sources have narrated that the Prophet ﷺ said: 'Verily the fasting person has a prayer that will never be rejected.' Thus, he used to pray for the good of this world and the hereafter. He broke his fast before praying *Salaat ul Maghreb* (the evening prayer). In one authentic *hadith* he said: 'If the night enters from here and slips away from there, then the faster should end his fast.'

The Prophet Muhammad travelled during Ramadan, fasting and then breaking his fast. In this regard, he gave the companions the choice of fasting or not while travelling. During battle, however, he ordered them to break their fasts, to enable them to fight. Here it would be recalled that the Great Battle of Badr was fought during the month of Ramadan. Then, Allah gave the Muslims a victory that has known no parallel since. Yet, the Prophet ﷺ broke his fast in two of his battles according to narrations by Umar ibn al Khattab and collected by Al Tirmidhi and Ahmad. The Prophet did not, however, specify the distance after which the fast should be broken. There are in fact no authentic accounts to prove this.

There were, observedly, times when the morning prayer, *al Fajr*, came and the Prophet was still in a state of impurity following sexual intercourse. He would, in those circumstances, perform the ritual bath and thereafter fast. In a related matter, he used to kiss some of his wives while he was fasting in Ramadan. He compared the kiss of the fasting person to the washing of the mouth.

On another level, the Prophet Muhammad ﷺ ruled that the person who broke his fast through a genuine act of forgetfulness was not required to make up that day's fast. He pointed out that it was Allah Almighty who had fed and given drink to that person. We have learnt from the prophetic traditions also that the things which invalidate one's fast are: eating, drinking, cupping, and vomiting. The Noble Quran explains that sexual intercourse nullifies fasting in the same way that eating and drinking does.

Among his practices also was that of retreat and seclusion during the last ten days of Ramadan. The Prophet ﷺ did this in order to attune his heart ever more with Allah and to free his mind from the concerns of the world. The gaze of his heart thus became entirely focused in the heavens.

During this time, he limited his contacts with people and intensified his supplication and prayers to Allah, the Lord of all Majesty and Glory. His heart, therefore, indulged purely in the contemplation of Allah's attributes and qualities. It reflected upon His clear signs in the universe and of Allah's creation in the heavens and the earth. With all this in mind, it would be very difficult to determine how much knowledge Prophet ﷺ acquired, or how much light was revealed to him, or how many realities were exposed to him. He was, without doubt, the most knowledgeable person about Allah, the most fearful of Him, and the one who trusted and depended upon Him the most. Indeed, he was the most pious of all men and sacrificed himself the most for the sake of Allah! May the peace and blessings of Allah be upon him as long as musk continues to give its sweet fragrance and as long as pigeons echo their mournful cries and nightingales sing out their melodies.

Lesson 2

Why was fasting ordained?

To Allah Almighty there are certain secrets in His laws, insights in His rulings and objectives in His creation. In these secrets, insights and objectives are things which minds perceive and others that confound human understanding. With regard to fasting, Allah declared: 'O you who have attained to faith! Fasting is ordained for you as it was ordained for those before you, so that you might remain conscious of God' (2:183).

يَٰٓأَيُّهَا ٱلَّذِينَ ءَامَنُوا۟ كُتِبَ عَلَيْكُمُ ٱلصِّيَامُ كَمَا كُتِبَ عَلَى ٱلَّذِينَ مِن قَبْلِكُمْ لَعَلَّكُمْ تَتَّقُونَ

Accordingly, fasting is the way to piety and the fear of God. The fasting person is thus among the closest people to Allah, be He exalted. The stomach of the faster becomes hungry while his heart is purified. When he breaks his fast and quenches his thirst, his eyes overflow with tears. The Prophet ﷺ said: 'O youth, whoever is able from among you to pay the dowry, then he should marry for it is the best way of restraining the eyes and protecting one's private parts. Whoever is unable to do so, he should fast because it will be for him a shield.'

Fasting narrows the food and blood arteries. They are known to be canals of the devils, hence fasting reduces their insinuations. It further weakens carnal desires, thoughts and temptations of disobedience. It lightens the spirit. Fasting reminds the individual of his brothers who are also fasting, some of whom are poor and needy. He empathizes with them and extends the hand of help to them.

Fasting is a school for the training of the soul, purification of the heart, lowering of the gaze and protection of the limbs. It is a secret between the servant and his Lord. In an authentic *hadith* the Prophet ﷺ said: 'Every act of the son of man is for himself except fasting; it is for Me and I shall reward it.' That is because only Allah knows the extent of one's fast. It is quite different from other forms of worship such as prayers, *Zakaat* (the poor due) and pilgrimage, all of which can be witnessed by others.

The righteous predecessors acknowledged fasting as a means of drawing closer to Allah. To many it was accepted as a sphere of competition and a season for goodness. They cried for happiness when it arrived and wept out of sadness when it departed. Our ancestors knew the essence of fasting; hence they loved Ramadan and made unparalleled efforts and sacrifices in it. They stayed up during its nights, bowing and prostrating themselves in tears and humility. They passed its days in remembrance, recitation, learning, propagation and giving counsel.

Fasting was a delight and source of internal peace for the early Muslims. It expanded their bosoms. Hence, they trained their spirits towards its objectives, purified their hearts with its teachings and disciplined their souls with its wisdom. Numerous accounts confirm that they used to sit with their Qurans in the mosques, reciting, crying and protecting their tongues and eyes from unlawful things.

Fasting ensures the unity of Muslims. They fast and break their fast at the same time. They feel the pangs of hunger and eat together in a spirit of brotherhood, love and devotion. Fasting atones for errors and wrong-doing. Hence the Prophet ﷺ said: 'From Jumu'ah to Jumu'ah, 'Umrah to 'Umrah, and Ramadan to Ramadan there is atonement for what occurred between them as long as no major sin was committed.'

From a physical point of view, fasting enhances bodily health. It gets rid of contaminated matter, eases the stomach, purifies the blood, eases the working of the heart, brightens the spirit, refines the soul and disciplines the character. When an individual fasts, his soul is humbled, his heart is subdued, his ambitions are curbed, and his carnal desires are dispelled. Thus, his prayers are answered because of his closeness to Allah.

There is a great secret in fasting: that is to worship Allah and seek His pleasure by submitting to His orders and surrendering to His laws by forsaking one's desires, food and drink. Fasting therefore represents the triumph of a Muslim over his desires and the predominance of a believer over his inner self. It is half of patience. Whoever is unable to fast without any good reason, will never master his self or conquer his desires.

On the whole, fasting is a great training for the soul, so that it would be able to bear hardship and carry out its great duties such as *jihad*, sacrifice and initiative. Thus when Saul wanted to fight his enemies, Allah tested his people with a river. Saul said to them: 'Behold, God will now try you by a river: he who shall drink of it will not belong to me, whereas he who shall refrain from tasting it – he, indeed, will belong to me; but forgiven shall be he who shall scoop up but a single handful' (2:249).

فَلَمَّا فَصَلَ طَالُوتُ بِالْجُنُودِ قَالَ إِنَّ اللَّهَ مُبْتَلِيكُم بِنَهَرٍ فَمَن شَرِبَ مِنْهُ فَلَيْسَ مِنِّي وَمَن لَّمْ يَطْعَمْهُ فَإِنَّهُ مِنِّي إِلَّا مَنِ اغْتَرَفَ غُرْفَةً بِيَدِهِ ۚ فَشَرِبُوا مِنْهُ إِلَّا قَلِيلًا مِّنْهُمْ ۚ فَلَمَّا جَاوَزَهُ هُوَ وَالَّذِينَ آمَنُوا مَعَهُ قَالُوا لَا طَاقَةَ لَنَا الْيَوْمَ بِجَالُوتَ وَجُنُودِهِ ۚ قَالَ الَّذِينَ يَظُنُّونَ أَنَّهُم مُّلَاقُو اللَّهِ كَم مِّن فِئَةٍ قَلِيلَةٍ غَلَبَتْ فِئَةً كَثِيرَةً بِإِذْنِ اللَّهِ ۗ وَاللَّهُ مَعَ الصَّابِرِينَ

Those who were patient and mastered their desires were successful. On the other extreme, those who worshipped their base desires turned their backs on the *jihad*.

The wisdom of fasting can thus be summarized in the following: that it realizes God-consciousness, submission to His orders and subjugation of one's desires. It ensures a triumph over self and the preparation of a Muslim for situations of sacrifice. It enables him to control his limbs and desires. It ensures good physical health and atones for wrong-doing. It brings about togetherness, brotherhood and a sense of empathy for those who are hungry and needy. And Allah knows best.

Lesson 3

The Majestic Quran and the month of Ramadan

The Quran loves Ramadan and Ramadan loves the Quran. They are two beloved friends. Allah Almighty says: 'It was the month of Ramadan in which the Quran was [first] bestowed from on high as a guidance unto man and a self-evident proof of that guidance, and as the standard by which to discern the true from the false' (2:185).

شَهْرُ رَمَضَانَ ٱلَّذِىٓ أُنزِلَ فِيهِ ٱلْقُرْءَانُ هُدًى لِّلنَّاسِ وَبَيِّنَٰتٍ مِّنَ ٱلْهُدَىٰ وَٱلْفُرْقَانِ فَمَن شَهِدَ مِنكُمُ ٱلشَّهْرَ فَلْيَصُمْهُ وَمَن كَانَ مَرِيضًا أَوْ عَلَىٰ سَفَرٍ فَعِدَّةٌ مِّنْ أَيَّامٍ أُخَرَ يُرِيدُ ٱللَّهُ بِكُمُ ٱلْيُسْرَ وَلَا يُرِيدُ بِكُمُ ٱلْعُسْرَ وَلِتُكْمِلُوا۟ ٱلْعِدَّةَ وَلِتُكَبِّرُوا۟ ٱللَّهَ عَلَىٰ مَا هَدَىٰكُمْ وَلَعَلَّكُمْ تَشْكُرُونَ

The entire Quran was sent down from the 'Preserved Tablet' to the heavens of the earth in the month of Ramadan. It was, therefore, an honour for this month that the Quran should be revealed in it. For this reason the Prophet ﷺ used to study the Quran with the angel Gabriel during Ramadan. He used to listen and reflect upon its meanings, recite it, live with its calls, allow his heart to roam in its fields and release all his love in its treasures.

The person who reads while fasting combines Ramadan with the Glorious Quran. He, therefore, lives this month with the Noble Book about which Allah says: 'All this We have expounded in this blessed divine writ which We have revealed unto thee, [O Muhammad,] so that men may ponder over its messages, and that those who are endowed with insight may take them to heart' (38:29).

$$كِتَابٌ أَنزَلْنَاهُ إِلَيْكَ مُبَارَكٌ لِّيَدَّبَّرُوا آيَاتِهِ وَلِيَتَذَكَّرَ أُوْلُوا الْأَلْبَابِ$$

'Will they not, then, ponder over this Quran? Or are there locks upon their hearts?' (47:24).

$$أَفَلَا يَتَدَبَّرُونَ الْقُرْآنَ أَمْ عَلَىٰ قُلُوبٍ أَقْفَالُهَا$$

'Will they not, then, try to understand this Quran? Had it issued from any but God, they would surely have found in it many an inner contradiction!' (4:82).

$$أَفَلَا يَتَدَبَّرُونَ الْقُرْآنَ وَلَوْ كَانَ مِنْ عِندِ غَيْرِ اللَّهِ لَوَجَدُوا فِيهِ اخْتِلَافًا كَثِيرًا$$

In Ramadan, the Noble Quran has its own special taste and flavour. It offers exceptional inspiration and distinct rationales. Still besides, the Quran bestows fresh vitality. Ramadan brings back memories of the Quran's revelation, its days of collective study, and the periods of attention devoted to it by our predecessors. The Prophet ﷺ once advised: 'Read the Quran for surely it will be an intercessor for you on the Day of Judgement.' He also said; 'The best of you are those who learn the Quran and teach it.' And:

'Read the two flowers, Surah al Baqarah and Al Imran. They will come as two clouds or as a barrier of crowded birds that would shade their readers on the Day of Judgement.'

The Prophet ﷺ also said: 'The one who reads the Quran and is expert in doing so will be with the noble and virtuous angels. And the one who reads the Quran and stutters with it, he will have two rewards.'

When Ramadan came, our forefathers used to disengage themselves and set out on a spiritual journey with the Glorious Quran. It was said that when Ramadan came Imam Malik never preoccupied himself except with the Quran. He used to suspend teaching and issuing legal rulings during this time, pointing out that this was the month of the Quran. And so the homes of our forebears had a special buzz as that of bees. Their homes radiated light and filled hearts with happiness. They used to recite the Quran in the most melodious voices, stopping at its wonders and crying because of its admonitions, becoming happy with its tidings, enjoining its commands and forbidding its prohibitions.

It was confirmed that Ibn Mas'ud once read the first part of Surah al Nisa for our Prophet until he reached the verse: 'How, then, [will the sinners fare on Judgement Day,] when We shall bring forward witnesses from within every community, and bring thee [O prophet] as witness against them?' (4:41).

فَكَيْفَ إِذَا جِئْنَا مِن كُلِّ أُمَّةٍ بِشَهِيدٍ وَجِئْنَا بِكَ عَلَىٰ هَـٰؤُلَاءِ شَهِيدًا

Then the Prophet ﷺ stopped him saying: 'That is enough for now.' Ibn Mas'ud said when he looked at the Prophet, his eyes were flowing with tears. Clearly it was the admirer hearing the words of his beloved and crying.

Still according to another account, the Prophet ﷺ once listened to Abi Musa reciting the Quran while the latter was unaware that he was being listened to. Then the Prophet ﷺ said to him: 'Did you not see me listening to your skilful recitation? You were given a flute from the flutes of David.' Abu Musa replied: 'If I knew, O Messenger of Allah that you were listening to me, I would have embellished it considerably.' Meaning that he would have beautified his voice more than ever, thereby making the Quran more effective, impressive and elegant.

In this context it was reported that when Umar ibn al Khattab sat with the companions he used to say: 'O Abu Musa! Remind us of our Lord.' The latter would surge forward and recite with his beautiful voice leaving them all crying.

Verily the listening to his words has caused me to cry, For how would it be if my eyes were to see Him manifest. He recited the remembrance of his Master and yearned to meet Him And the longing of the hearts of those who know Him are renewed.

When the whims of later generations turned them away from listening to the words of Allah, learning became distorted, dispositions were turned upside down and understandings became afflicted.

When the Quran was substituted by other sources of guidance, corruption became common, calamities multiplied, understandings were thrown into disarray and fortitude disappeared. Surely the purpose of the Quran is to guide people to the straight path. It is a light and remedy for the illnesses of the heart. It is knowledge, culture and evidence. The Quran is life, spirit, salvation, happiness, reward and recompense. It is a divine teaching, a constitution and eternal wisdom.

Will we not then live with the Quran in Ramadan and outside of Ramadan? Will we not recognize the greatness of the Quran and fill our hearts with its happiness, and radiance? Will we not do this?

Lesson 4

The chants of those who fast

There are to the people who fast certain special melodies, cherished songs and unceasing chants. Those who fast are the most conscious of Allah. They remember Him always with by saying: 'Glory be to Allah (Subhanallah), all praise is due Allah (Alhamdulillah), Allah is the greatest (Allahu Akbar), and I ask Allah for forgiveness (Astagfirullah)'. If the day becomes long for the fasting, they make it shorter with their constant remembrance of Allah. If the pangs of hunger pain them, they overcome this through the remembrance of Allah. They find delight in their remembrance and happiness. They remember Allah and He remembers them. 'So remember Me, and I shall remember you' (2:152).

فَاذْكُرُونِي أَذْكُرْكُمْ وَاشْكُرُوا لِي وَلَا تَكْفُرُونِ

Likewise, when they give thanks and show gratitude to Him, He increases His favour upon them. 'If you are grateful [to Me], I shall most certainly give you more and more' (14:7).

وَإِذْ تَأَذَّنَ رَبُّكُمْ لَئِن شَكَرْتُمْ لَأَزِيدَنَّكُمْ وَلَئِن كَفَرْتُمْ إِنَّ عَذَابِي لَشَدِيدٌ

The truthful fasters remember Allah standing, sitting and reclining on their sides. Their hearts become contented with the remembrance of Allah, their spirits become happy with love for Allah, their souls become relaxed with the longing to meet Allah. Prophet Muhammad ﷺ said: 'The example of the one who remembers Allah and the one who does not remember Him is like the living and the dead.' There are many dead people who do not know the remembrance of Allah. They live, eat, drink, roam freely and rejoice. Yet they absolutely do not know life.

It was reported that the Prophet ﷺ said: 'Those who are singled out will arrive before others.' The companions asked, 'Who are they that are singled out?' He replied, 'The men and women who remember Allah often.' The fasting person who remembers Allah is foremost in doing good. Such a one is close to Paradise and far from the fire of Hell. His records are filled with good deeds and overflowing with righteousness. Congratulations and best wishes to him.

Toward this end, a man asked the Prophet to inform him of a deed that he should cling to. Allah's Messenger told him: 'Keep your tongue always moistened with the remembrance of Allah.'

The following poem (written originally in Arabic) is an excellent expression of this sublime reverence. It reflects the peak of ingenuity. It tells of how a fasting person becomes hungry and yet always remembers Allah. How he thirsts and yet continues to glorify Allah:

> Remember us as we remember You, perhaps remembrance will shorten the distance.
>
> Remember the searcher when he crosses Your path, shedding tears and yearning for happiness.

Those who remember Allah much, often do so with the exhaling of their breath, the meeting of their lips and the succession of every moment. They secure with their contemplation the greatest rewards, highest aspirations and most generous sacrifice. If some of the negligent turn away from the remembrance of Allah, they will be overcome by anxiety and trapped by distress and sadness. Surely they have the remedy, but they do not take it. They have the cure but they do not know it. 'Verily, in the remembrance of [God] men's hearts do find their rest' (13:28).

ٱلَّذِينَ ءَامَنُوا۟ وَتَطْمَئِنُّ قُلُوبُهُم بِذِكْرِ ٱللَّهِ أَلَا بِذِكْرِ ٱللَّهِ تَطْمَئِنُّ ٱلْقُلُوبُ

The Prophet ﷺ said: 'Whoever says glory and praise be to Allah, a date tree shall be planted for him in Paradise.' How many date trees, therefore, have eluded the people who indulge in heavy sleep and long hours of folly?

> Will you feel sorry for the one who insists on wrong-doing,
>
> Will you show mercy to him but you show no mercy to yourself?
>
> You shun me always because of my thoughtlessness, And yet you spent your life in negligence.

Still on the virtues of God consciousness, the Prophet ﷺ said: 'I prefer to say glory be to Allah, praise to Allah, there is no God save Allah, and Allah is the greatest, than to have all that the sun ever shone upon.' And what is this world anyway? Of what value is its gold, silver and palaces? This is how the Prophet ﷺ weighed and valued them. For all that the sun ever shone upon is not equal to 'glory be to Allah, praise to Allah, there is no God save Allah, and Allah is the greatest'. Is there not a conscious being who would fill his hours with these precious words so that he may find them on the Day of the Greatest Presentation a source of light, pleasure and happiness?

The Prophet ﷺ said: 'Shall I not inform you of your best and most precious deeds before your Master? It is better for you than to spend gold and money. It is better for you than to meet your enemy and you smite their necks and they smite your necks?' The companions said: 'Yes, tell us O Messenger of Allah.' He said: 'The remembrance of God Almighty.'

Whenever the righteous predecessors prayed *al Fajr*, the morning prayer, they used to sit and remember Allah until day broke. Some used to spread their copies of the Quran after the morning prayer and devote their entire beings to the study of the signs and momentous rulings. They would fill their bosoms with light and their records with rewards. The one who has suffered the worst kind of losses is he whom Ramadan passes and who does not attain happiness in it from the remembrance of his Lord and does not spend his time in glorifying his Master. Is there not, therefore, a diligent one who would seize every breath of his life and minutes of time?

Lesson 5

Ramadan is a school for the learning of generosity and scarifice

Allah Almighty says: 'For whatever good deed you may offer up in your own behalf, you shall truly find it with God' (73:20).

إِنَّ رَبَّكَ يَعْلَمُ أَنَّكَ تَقُومُ أَدْنَىٰ مِن ثُلُثَىِ ٱلَّيْلِ وَنِصْفَهُ وَثُلُثَهُ وَطَآئِفَةٌ مِّنَ ٱلَّذِينَ مَعَكَ وَٱللَّهُ يُقَدِّرُ ٱلَّيْلَ وَٱلنَّهَارَ عَلِمَ أَن لَّن تُحْصُوهُ فَتَابَ عَلَيْكُمْ فَٱقْرَءُوا۟ مَا تَيَسَّرَ مِنَ ٱلْقُرْءَانِ عَلِمَ أَن سَيَكُونُ مِنكُم مَّرْضَىٰ وَءَاخَرُونَ يَضْرِبُونَ فِى ٱلْأَرْضِ يَبْتَغُونَ مِن فَضْلِ ٱللَّهِ وَءَاخَرُونَ يُقَٰتِلُونَ فِى سَبِيلِ ٱللَّهِ فَٱقْرَءُوا۟ مَا تَيَسَّرَ مِنْهُ وَأَقِيمُوا۟ ٱلصَّلَوٰةَ وَءَاتُوا۟ ٱلزَّكَوٰةَ وَأَقْرِضُوا۟ ٱللَّهَ قَرْضًا حَسَنًا وَمَا تُقَدِّمُوا۟ لِأَنفُسِكُم مِّنْ خَيْرٍ تَجِدُوهُ عِندَ ٱللَّهِ هُوَ خَيْرًا وَأَعْظَمَ أَجْرًا وَٱسْتَغْفِرُوا۟ ٱللَّهَ إِنَّ ٱللَّهَ غَفُورٌ رَّحِيمٌ

He also says: 'The parable of those who spend their possessions for the sake of God is that of a grain out of which grow seven ears, in every ear a hundred grains: for God grants manifold increase unto whom He wills; and God is infinite, all-knowing' (2:261).

$$\text{مَثَلُ ٱلَّذِينَ يُنفِقُونَ أَمْوَٰلَهُمْ فِى سَبِيلِ ٱللَّهِ كَمَثَلِ حَبَّةٍ أَنۢبَتَتْ سَبْعَ سَنَابِلَ فِى كُلِّ سُنۢبُلَةٍ مِّا۟ئَةُ حَبَّةٍ وَٱللَّهُ يُضَٰعِفُ لِمَن يَشَآءُ وَٱللَّهُ وَٰسِعٌ عَلِيمٌ}$$

In an authentic *hadith*, Ibn Abbas narrated that the Prophet ﷺ was naturally the most generous of people and that he used to be more generous than ever in the month of Ramadan when Gabriel met him. Indeed, he used to be more generous than a blessed wind. Fasting calls for the feeding of the hungry, giving to the indigent and offering to the poor. Ramadan is a season for the open-handed, a well-timed opportunity for those who sacrifice and give. Allah has given you, so sacrifice out of what he has given you, for wealth is a loan for exchange, and life is a traveller. Wealth is like water, if its flow is obstructed it becomes brackish, and if it flows, it becomes sweet and fresh.

What sublime sacrifice, what excellent charity, what beautiful offering. The Prophet ﷺ said: 'Verily Allah has two angels who call every morning. One says: "O Allah give the generous a replacement for what he spent." The other angel would say: "O Allah give the miserly wastage."

Thus, every time a servant of Allah gives something in charity Allah eases his physical, spiritual and mental conditions. And He expands for him his sustenance. The Prophet ﷺ said: 'Charity extinguishes a wrong as water puts out fire.' Wrong-doings create a heat in the hearts and a flame in the souls, and a burning fire in life. Only charity can put out this blazing fire. Indeed, charity is a cooling for the heart and a fragrance for the spirit, erasing in the most complete way every wrong-doing.

Here again, the Prophet ﷺ said: 'Every person will be in the shade of his charity on the Day of Judgement, until all matters are settled between the people.' This is truly astonishing: that charity should have an expansive shade and shadows in which the servants of Allah shade themselves on the Day of Judgement; each one according to the shade that was produced by his charity in this world.

The third Righteously Guided Caliph, Uthman ibn Affan, was very rich. He used his wealth and vast possessions to gain the pleasure of Allah by equipping the Muslim army before it set out for the Battle of Tabuk. He bought an entire well especially for the Muslims. He will certainly be rewarded for his generosity and sacrifice. Abdur Rahman ibn Awf was another wealthy companion. On one occasion he gave to the poor people of Madinah, for the sake of Allah, the merchandise of an entire caravan comprising 700 camels.

- There are people who fast and do not have a piece of bread, or a taste of milk or a handful of dates.
- There are others who fast and do not have a house to shelter themselves, or means of transport to convey them, or a friend to support them.

- Still besides, there are other people who fast and do not have anything to eat before or after their fast.

In this context the Prophet ﷺ said: 'Whoever feeds a fasting person he will have the same reward like him, without there being any reduction in the reward of the one who is fasting.' Hence, the generosity of righteous people is increased in Ramadan. They give, spend and sacrifice. Many of them usually provide meals for gatherings of poor Muslims to break their fast each day in Ramadan. By so doing, they seek a great and abundant reward from Allah Almighty.

The mosques of our righteous predecessors used to be filled with food provided for the poor; to the extent that one could not find a hungry or needy person. Of course, it is quite amazing that all which a servant spends of his food, drink and clothes is of no consequence except that which was spent seeking the pleasure of Allah, the Sublime. He says in the Quran: 'If you offer up to God a goodly loan, He will amply repay you for it, and will forgive you your sins: for God is ever responsive to gratitude, forbearing' (64:17).

إِن تُقْرِضُوا ٱللَّهَ قَرْضًا حَسَنًا يُضَٰعِفْهُ لَكُمْ وَيَغْفِرْ لَكُمْ وَٱللَّهُ شَكُورٌ حَلِيمٌ

O fasting person, know that by your sacrifice and giving you are actually giving a loan to your Lord for the day of your poverty and need. The Day of Indigence and Wretchedness. The Day of Loss and Gain. O fasting person, know that a drink of water, a taste of milk, a handful of dates, the little food, money, clothes and fruits that you give to the needy are all it takes to clear your way to Paradise. O fasting person, know by Allah, that nothing preserves wealth like charity. Nothing purifies wealth like the *Zakaat*. Many rich people have died and left wealth and treasures, tall buildings and palaces, the quantity of which only Allah knows. Yet, all of it became a source of regret and sorrow; because they never used their wealth in the right way. Tomorrow you will see the winners and the losers, and surely help is only from Allah.

Lesson 6

Ramadan: the month of standing up at night

'O thou enwrapped one! Keep awake [in prayer] at night, all but a small part. Of half thereof or make it a little less than that, or add to it [at will]; and [during that time] recite the Quran calmly and distinctly, with thy mind attuned to its meaning' (73:1–3).

يَـٰٓأَيُّهَا ٱلْمُزَّمِّلُ ۝ قُمِ ٱلَّيْلَ إِلَّا قَلِيلًا ۝ نِّصْفَهُۥٓ أَوِ ٱنقُصْ مِنْهُ قَلِيلًا

This is what Allah Almighty said to His Prophet. And, naturally, the noble messenger complied with the command of His Lord by standing long hours at night, crying profusely in all humiliation.

In the same manner, Allah ordered his beloved Prophet ﷺ: 'And rise from thy sleep and pray during part of the night [as well], as a free offering from thee, and thy Sustainer may well raise thee to a glorious station [in the life to come]' (17:79).

وَمِنَ ٱلَّيْلِ فَتَهَجَّدْ بِهِۦ نَافِلَةً لَّكَ عَسَىٰٓ أَن يَبْعَثَكَ رَبُّكَ مَقَامًا مَّحْمُودًا

Accordingly, in the same manner that your standing at night in this world will be glorious and honoured so too will it be on the Day of Judgement.

Ramadan is the month of fasting and standing at night. The sweetest nights and most precious hours are when the fasting people stand in the darkness of night.

I said to the night, is there a secret in your depth?
Filled with conversation and unknown matters.

It said: I never throughout my life encountered
finer words, than the words of my
beloved in the early hours of the morning.

The nights of the fasting people are short because they are delightful. On the other extreme, the nights of the frivolous are long because they are unhealthy. The short ones are thus accompanied by extended concerns while the long ones contain momentary pleasures. Allah Almighty describes His righteous servants thus: 'They would lie asleep during but a small part of the night' (51:17).

كَانُوا۟ قَلِيلًا مِّنَ ٱلَّيْلِ مَا يَهْجَعُونَ

And: 'In the hours of early dawn they were found praying for forgiveness' (51:18).

وَبِٱلْأَسْحَارِ هُمْ يَسْتَغْفِرُونَ

And: 'Those who pray for forgiveness in the early hours of the morning' (3:17).

ٱلصَّٰبِرِينَ وَٱلصَّٰدِقِينَ وَٱلْقَٰنِتِينَ وَٱلْمُنفِقِينَ وَٱلْمُسْتَغْفِرِينَ بِٱلْأَسْحَارِ

The sound of weeping used to be heard from among the Prophet's companions, Migrants (*Muhajirun*) and Helpers

(*Ansars*), whenever the darkness of night descended upon them. And, when day broke, they would become like bold and fearless lions. In other words they were like monks at night but when they met their enemies at day they were the bravest of the brave. The homes of the companions were, in fact, schools for training and the learning of how to recite the Quran. They became institutes of faith. Today the homes of many people have become barracks for music, vice, and refuges of perversion. May Allah save us from such evils.

When we lost the standing in prayer at night, our hearts became hard. Our tears dried up and our faith became weak. The Prophet ﷺ said: 'Whoever stands the nights of Ramadan in faith and consciousness, all the sins which he sent forth will be forgiven.' Among the things that help one to stand at night in prayer is the calling to mind of the Momentous Day: when people will stand before the Lord of the worlds. The day when the graves will turn out their contents and all that were buried in bosoms will be revealed.

There are besides, other factors that help in standing at night. They include remembrance of the great reward and forgiveness of sins and wrong-doing. The righteous predecessors preoccupied themselves with standing at night. Among them were those who spent the nights bowing, prostrating themselves or standing before Allah. Among them were those who recited crying, who contemplated and hoped, and who were thankful and considerate. For why have you made your homes desolate places without any standing and praying at night? Why have you made it empty of Quranic recitations? Why have our homes complained because of the lack of prayers in them at night?

If nights set in, the hearts of the negligent sleep and the spirits of the playful die while the hearts of the believers come to life with wide awakened and fearful eyes. How can one who remembers the repose of the grave, the gathering of mankind and the decisive manifestation ever sleep? Surely no one ever expected that a generation of Muslims would spend their nights shamelessly in playing chess and listening to music. The Prophet ﷺ said: 'O servant of Allah, do not be like such and such a person. He used to stand in prayer at nights and then he abandoned this practice.'

Lesson 7

The Islamic home in Ramadan

Allah, the Exalted and Power says: 'Which then, is better: he who has founded his building on God-consciousness and [a desire for] His goodly acceptance – or he who has founded his building on the edge of a water-worn, crumbling river-bank, so that it [is bound to] tumble down with him into the fire of hell? For God does not grace with His guidance people who [deliberately] do wrong' (9:109).

أَفَمَنْ أَسَّسَ بُنْيَـٰنَهُۥ عَلَىٰ تَقْوَىٰ مِنَ ٱللَّهِ وَرِضْوَٰنٍ خَيْرٌ أَم مَّنْ أَسَّسَ بُنْيَـٰنَهُۥ عَلَىٰ شَفَا جُرُفٍ هَارٍ فَٱنْهَارَ بِهِۦ فِى نَارِ جَهَنَّمَ وَٱللَّهُ لَا يَهْدِى ٱلْقَوْمَ ٱلظَّـٰلِمِينَ

The Islamic home is one that is founded on God-consciousness. Its pillars are the fear of Allah. Its foundations are good deeds; its garden is obedience to the commands of Allah. He says: 'O you who have attained to faith! Ward off from yourselves and those who are close to you that fire [of the hereafter] whose fuel is human beings and stones: [lording] over it are angelic powers awesome [and] severe'

(66:6).

$$\text{يَا أَيُّهَا الَّذِينَ آمَنُوا قُوا أَنفُسَكُمْ وَأَهْلِيكُمْ نَارًا وَقُودُهَا النَّاسُ وَالْحِجَارَةُ عَلَيْهَا مَلَائِكَةٌ غِلَاظٌ شِدَادٌ لَا يَعْصُونَ اللَّهَ مَا أَمَرَهُمْ وَيَفْعَلُونَ مَا يُؤْمَرُونَ}$$

The home is a trust, a responsibility and a stewardship. Are there not shepherds who are conscious of their flock? The Prophet ﷺ said: 'Every one of you is a shepherd and each one of you is responsible for that which is under his care.' The stewardship of the home in Ramadan and out of Ramadan entails the ordering of its members to pray. Allah Almighty says: 'He used to enjoin upon his people prayer and charity, and found favour in his Sustainer's sight' (19:55).

$$\text{وَكَانَ يَأْمُرُ أَهْلَهُ بِالصَّلَاةِ وَالزَّكَاةِ وَكَانَ عِندَ رَبِّهِ مَرْضِيًّا}$$

The most pressing need of a Muslim home is an upright father and believing mother who undertake the upbringing of their offspring. 'Behold, God bids you to deliver all that you have been entrusted with unto those who are entitled thereto' (4:58).

$$\text{إِنَّ اللَّهَ يَأْمُرُكُمْ أَن تُؤَدُّوا الْأَمَانَاتِ إِلَىٰ أَهْلِهَا وَإِذَا حَكَمْتُم بَيْنَ النَّاسِ أَن تَحْكُمُوا بِالْعَدْلِ إِنَّ اللَّهَ نِعِمَّا يَعِظُكُم بِهِ إِنَّ اللَّهَ كَانَ سَمِيعًا بَصِيرًا}$$

Surely among the greatest trusts is that of improving the home. The Islamic home, therefore, passes Ramadan in remembrance, recitation, humility and fear of Allah. It is filled with the traditions of the Prophet Muhammad ﷺ in food and drink, coming and going, sleeping and waking. The Islamic home respects and observes the ethics of separation and covering. It worships Allah through this means and considers it a source of honour and dignity for the Muslim woman. Allah will reward its observance abundantly. Many homes have been tested with wealth. It corrupted the hearts of its members, ruined their future and undermined their power.

When wealth entered some homes, remembrance, inner peace, shame and dignity departed from them. Allah says: 'But among men there is many a one that prefers a mere play with words [to divine guidance], so as to lead [those] without knowledge astray from the path of God' (31:6).

$$\text{وَمِنَ ٱلنَّاسِ مَن يَشْتَرِى لَهْوَ ٱلْحَدِيثِ لِيُضِلَّ عَن سَبِيلِ ٱللَّهِ بِغَيْرِ عِلْمٍ وَيَتَّخِذَهَا هُزُوًا أُوْلَٰٓئِكَ لَهُمْ عَذَابٌ مُّهِينٌ}$$

According to the scholars the play with words here refers to music. How many examples are there in which music has abused values, derided principles and exhausted minds? The Islamic home arises with the remembrance of Allah and sleeps with His remembrance, far from vain and idle talk. The Noble Quran describes them as those 'who turn away from all that is frivolous' (23:3).

$$\text{وَٱلَّذِينَ هُمْ عَنِ ٱللَّغْوِ مُعْرِضُونَ}$$

The Islamic home has a sense of shame before Allah. Hence the Prophet ﷺ said: 'O people, be chaste and modest before Allah. And true modesty before Allah is to control one's mind and its consciousness, to protect one's stomach and that which it collects and whoever remembers the trials will abandon the ornaments of life and this world.'

O how good it would be if the knowledge of religion were to enter the precincts of our Islamic homes to become gardens for forgiveness and acknowledgement. The home is in dire need of some important features. Foremost among them is the establishment of the five prayers at their appointed times bowing and prostrating in humility and spirituality. It needs also the recitation of the Quran during the night and at the extremes of the day. It needs the remembrance of Allah at daybreak and at dusk. It needs the revival of the traditions of the Prophet ﷺ at every moment and opportunity. And it needs the expulsion of every folly and the avoidance of vain talk and bearing of false witness. Allah Almighty says: 'Behold, as for those who say, "Our Sustainer is God", and then steadfastly pursue the right way – upon them do angels often descend, [saying:] "Fear not and grieve not, but receive the glad tidings of that Paradise which has been promised to you!"' (41:30).

إِنَّ ٱلَّذِينَ قَالُوا۟ رَبُّنَا ٱللَّهُ ثُمَّ ٱسْتَقَٰمُوا۟ تَتَنَزَّلُ عَلَيْهِمُ ٱلْمَلَٰٓئِكَةُ أَلَّا تَخَافُوا۟ وَلَا تَحْزَنُوا۟ وَأَبْشِرُوا۟ بِٱلْجَنَّةِ ٱلَّتِى كُنتُمْ تُوعَدُونَ

And: 'God grants firmness unto those who have attained to faith through the word that is unshakeably true in the life of this world as well as in the life to come; but the wrongdoers He lets go astray: for God does whatever He wills' (14:27).

يُثَبِّتُ ٱللَّهُ ٱلَّذِينَ ءَامَنُوا۟ بِٱلْقَوْلِ ٱلثَّابِتِ فِى ٱلْحَيَوٰةِ ٱلدُّنْيَا وَفِى ٱلْءَاخِرَةِ وَيُضِلُّ ٱللَّهُ ٱلظَّٰلِمِينَ وَيَفْعَلُ ٱللَّهُ مَا يَشَآءُ

Surely the month of Ramadan bestows upon the Muslim home spirituality and satisfaction. It awakens its members to stand in prayer at nights, beckons them to fast in the day, and encourages them to remember Allah the Exalted.

'It is they who [truly] follow God's revelation, and are constant in prayer, and spend on others, secretly and openly, out of what We provide for them as sustenance – it is they who may look forward to a bargain that can never fail, since He will grant them their just rewards, and give them yet more out of His bounty: for, verily, He is much-forgiving, ever-responsive to gratitude' (35:29–30).

إِنَّ ٱلَّذِينَ يَتْلُونَ كِتَٰبَ ٱللَّهِ وَأَقَامُوا۟ ٱلصَّلَوٰةَ وَأَنفَقُوا۟ مِمَّا رَزَقْنَٰهُمْ سِرًّا وَعَلَانِيَةً يَرْجُونَ تِجَٰرَةً لَّن تَبُورَ ۝ لِيُوَفِّيَهُمْ أُجُورَهُمْ وَيَزِيدَهُم مِّن فَضْلِهِۦٓ ۚ إِنَّهُۥ غَفُورٌ شَكُورٌ

We ask You Who is the most merciful of those who show mercy to fill our homes with faith, wisdom and tranquillity.

Lesson 8

How does the heart fast?

'And if anyone believes in Allah, (Allah) guides his heart (aright)' (64:11).

مَآ أَصَابَ مِن مُّصِيبَةٍ إِلَّا بِإِذْنِ ٱللَّهِۗ وَمَن يُؤْمِنۢ بِٱللَّهِ يَهْدِ قَلْبَهُۥۚ وَٱللَّهُ بِكُلِّ شَىْءٍ عَلِيمٌ

The guidance of the heart is the basis of all guidance, the law of all success, the origin of every deed and head of every action. The Prophet ﷺ said: 'Truly there is a piece of flesh in the body which, if it be wholesome, the whole body will be healthy and which, and if it be diseased the whole body will be diseased. Truly it is the heart.'

Thus the goodness of your heart is the guarantee of your happiness in this world and in the hereafter. Likewise, its corruption is the surest way to destruction, the extent of which only Allah knows. 'In this, behold, there is indeed a reminder for everyone whose heart is wide-awake – that is [everyone who] lends ear with a conscious mind' (50:37).

إِنَّ فِى ذَٰلِكَ لَذِكْرَىٰ لِمَن كَانَ لَهُۥ قَلْبٌ أَوْ أَلْقَى ٱلسَّمْعَ وَهُوَ شَهِيدٌ

Every creature has a heart. In reality though they are two hearts, a heart that is alive and pulsating with the light of faith. It is filled with intense conviction and God-consciousness. The other is a dead heart, covered and diseased with every wreckage and rubbish.

Allah Almighty says concerning the hearts of the foolish folk: 'In their hearts is disease, and so God lets their disease increase' (2:10).

هَلْ يَنظُرُونَ إِلَّا أَن يَأْتِيَهُمُ ٱللَّهُ فِى ظُلَلٍ مِّنَ ٱلْغَمَامِ وَٱلْمَلَٰٓئِكَةُ وَقُضِىَ ٱلْأَمْرُ وَإِلَى ٱللَّهِ تُرْجَعُ ٱلْأُمُورُ

'But they say, "Our hearts are already full of knowledge." Nay, but God has rejected them because of their refusal to acknowledge the truth: for, few are the things in which they believe' (2:88).

وَقَالُوا۟ قُلُوبُنَا غُلْفٌۢ بَل لَّعَنَهُمُ ٱللَّهُ بِكُفْرِهِمْ فَقَلِيلًا مَّا يُؤْمِنُونَ

Allah also says: 'Will they not, then, ponder over this Quran? – or are there locks upon their hearts?' (47:24).

أَفَلَا يَتَدَبَّرُونَ ٱلْقُرْءَانَ أَمْ عَلَىٰ قُلُوبٍ أَقْفَالُهَآ

'And so they say, [as it were:] "Our hearts are veiled from whatever thou callest us to, [O Muhammad,] and in our ears is deafness"' (41:5).

وَقَالُوا۟ قُلُوبُنَا فِىٓ أَكِنَّةٍ مِّمَّا تَدْعُونَآ إِلَيْهِ وَفِىٓ ءَاذَانِنَا وَقْرٌ وَمِنۢ بَيْنِنَا وَبَيْنِكَ حِجَابٌ فَٱعْمَلْ إِنَّنَا عَٰمِلُونَ

From all these verses we learn that the hearts can become ill, they can be covered, locked and they die. The enemies of Allah have hearts in their bosoms but they do not perceive with these hearts. Hence the Prophet ﷺ used to say: 'O dispenser of hearts make my heart firm in Your religion.'

The heart of the believer fasts during Ramadan and outside of Ramadan. The fasting of the heart is done by emptying it of all corrupt material such as destructive forms of polytheism, false beliefs, evil suggestions, filthy intentions and degenerate thoughts. The heart of the believer is adorned with the love of Allah. It knows its Lord by His names and His qualities as He has described Himself. This heart explores with a discerning eye the lines of His names and qualities and the pages of Allah's making in the universe and the books of His creations.

The believer's heart is filled with a brilliant light which does not allow any darkness to remain with it. It is the light of the eternal message, the divine teachings, and the omnipotent laws. To it is added the natural light upon which the servants of Allah were created. Thus two great lights come together. 'Light upon light! God guides unto His light him that wills [to be guided]; and [to this end] God propounds parables unto men, since God [alone] has full knowledge of all things' (24:36).

فِى بُيُوتٍ أَذِنَ ٱللَّهُ أَن تُرْفَعَ وَيُذْكَرَ فِيهَا ٱسْمُهُۥ يُسَبِّحُ لَهُۥ فِيهَا بِٱلْغُدُوِّ وَٱلْآصَالِ

The believer's heart glows like a lamp, shines like the sun and sparkles like the morning light. It increases in faith whenever the believer listens to the verses of the Quran, it grows in conviction when it contemplates, and increases in guidance when it reflects. The believer's heart abstains from pride because it breaks its fast. Pride does not reside in the heart of a believer because it is unlawful. The abode and dwelling place of pride is the heart. Hence, if it enters any heart, that person will become afflicted, foolish, arrogant and frivolous.

Allah Almighty says in a *hadith* Qudsi: 'Pride is my upper garment and grandeur is my lower one, whoever contests with me for them I will punish him.' The Prophet ﷺ himself said: 'Whoever shows arrogance to Allah, He will humble him, and whoever is humble to Allah, He will raise him in station.'

The heart of the believer fasts and abstains from egotism. Egotism is when the individual sees himself as perfect, better than others and in possession of good qualities that are not found in anyone else. This is destruction in its most naked form. The Prophet ﷺ said: 'Three things which are totally destructive: a person's self-centredness and conceit, his reluctance to obey and his following of his desires.' The cure for this self-importance is to look at one's own faults, one's many shortcomings, thousands of sins and misdeeds that one has committed, wrongs that one has done and forgotten but the knowledge of which are with Allah in a book. For Allah is not led astray nor does He forget.

The heart of the believer fasts and abstains from envy because it lowers righteous deeds, puts out the light of the heart and stops its progress toward Allah the Most High. Allah says in the Glorious Quran: 'Do they, perchance, envy other people for what God has granted them out of his bounty? (4:54).

أَمْ يَحْسُدُونَ ٱلنَّاسَ عَلَىٰ مَآ ءَاتَىٰهُمُ ٱللَّهُ مِن فَضْلِهِۦ ۖ فَقَدْ ءَاتَيْنَآ ءَالَ إِبْرَٰهِيمَ ٱلْكِتَٰبَ وَٱلْحِكْمَةَ وَءَاتَيْنَٰهُم مُّلْكًا عَظِيمًا

And the Prophet ﷺ said: 'Do not envy one another; do not inflate prices one to another; do not hate one another; do not turn away from one another; and do not undercut one another.'

The Prophet informed one of his companions three times that he would be among the people of Paradise. When he was asked about what was it that earned him a place in Paradise, the man said: 'I do not sleep with envy, grudge or deceit in my heart for any Muslim.' Are there any hearts that would, therefore, fast like the learned. The fast of the learned has a yearning for the Most Merciful Lord of the worlds. Their hearts fast at all times and in the early hours of morning they seek forgiveness.

O Allah guide our hearts to the straight path and make it firm on faith, O Lord of the worlds.

Lesson 9

How does the tongue fast?

The tongue has a special fast. It is well known to those believers who turn away from all that is frivolous. The fasting of the tongue is a permanent feature of Ramadan and out of Ramadan, though in Ramadan the tongue is disciplined and curbed. The Prophet ﷺ said: 'Control this' and he pointed to his tongue. In response, Mu'adh said: 'Even if we start to speak about what we should. O Messenger of Allah?' The Prophet replied: 'Your mother would grieve for you O Mu'adh, will people not be thrown into the fire on their faces only because of the fruits of their tongues.'

The harm of the tongue is great and its danger is huge. Abu Bakr al Siddiq used to hold on to his tongue and say: 'This is what landed me in this position.' The tongue has seven injuries, the serpent bites and fire burns. Do not mention the faults of people with your tongues. For all of you have faults and the people have tongues.

Ibn Abbas used to say to his tongue: 'O tongue! Say something good and gain, or abstain from evil and be safe.'

Allah had shown mercy to a Muslim who restrained his tongue from treachery, averted it from backbiting, prevented it from vain talk, and barred it from prohibitions. Surely Allah will be merciful to he who checks his utterances and weighs his words. He says in the Quran: 'Not even a word can he utter but there is a watcher with him, ever-present' (50:18).

$$\text{مَا يَلْفِظُ مِن قَوْلٍ إِلَّا لَدَيْهِ رَقِيبٌ عَتِيدٌ}$$

Every expression is recorded and every word is counted. 'And never does Allah the least wrong to His creatures' (41:46).

$$\text{مَنْ عَمِلَ صَالِحًا فَلِنَفْسِهِ ۖ وَمَنْ أَسَاءَ فَعَلَيْهَا ۗ وَمَا رَبُّكَ بِظَلَّامٍ لِلْعَبِيدِ}$$

In this regard the Prophet ﷺ said: 'Whoever can protect for me what is between his jaws and between his legs, I will guarantee for him a place in Paradise.'

When the righteous predecessors disciplined themselves with the morality of the Quran and Sunnah, they weighed their utterances and respected their words. Their pronouncements were the remembrances of Allah, their looks were lessons, and their silence thought. When these righteous people feared the meeting with their Lord, the One, the Subduer, they used their tongues in His remembrance and gratefulness. And they refrained from treachery, obscenity and prattle. Ibn Mas'ud said: 'By Allah, there is not anything more deserving than the extended control of the tongue.' The righteous need words, they remember its consequences and results and they keep quiet.

How can someone fast and and give free rein to his tongue? How can someone fast and his tongue plays with him, his words deceive him and his logic misleads him? How can someone fast and lie, backbite, revile, abuse others and forget the Day of Judgement? How can someone be considered to be fasting while he bears false witness and does not cease from hurting Muslims? The Prophet ﷺ said: 'A Muslim is he from whose tongue and hands other Muslims are safe.' Is Islam anything other than deeds, practice, methodology, submission, behaviour and application? In the Glorious Quran Allah declares: 'Tell my servants that they should speak in the most kindly manner [unto those who do not share their beliefs]: verily, Satan is always ready to stir up discord between men – for, verily, Satan is man's open foe!' (17:54).

رَّبُّكُمْ أَعْلَمُ بِكُمْ إِن يَشَأْ يَرْحَمْكُمْ أَوْ إِن يَشَأْ يُعَذِّبْكُمْ وَمَآ أَرْسَلْنَٰكَ عَلَيْهِمْ وَكِيلًا

Surely the 'kindly manner' encouraged here is the good word that does not hurt any individual or group. It is the excellent speech that does not violate the honour of a Muslim or the dignity of a believer. 'And neither allow yourselves to speak ill of one another, and neither allow yourselves to speak ill of one another behind their backs. Would any of you like to eat the flesh of his dead brother? Nay, you would loathe it!' (49:12).

يَٰٓأَيُّهَا ٱلَّذِينَ ءَامَنُوا۟ ٱجْتَنِبُوا۟ كَثِيرًا مِّنَ ٱلظَّنِّ إِنَّ بَعْضَ ٱلظَّنِّ إِثْمٌ وَلَا تَجَسَّسُوا۟ وَلَا يَغْتَب بَّعْضُكُم بَعْضًا أَيُحِبُّ أَحَدُكُمْ أَن يَأْكُلَ لَحْمَ أَخِيهِ مَيْتًا فَكَرِهْتُمُوهُ وَٱتَّقُوا۟ ٱللَّهَ إِنَّ ٱللَّهَ تَوَّابٌ رَّحِيمٌ

How many fasting people spoilt their fasts when they debased their tongues, misused their reasoning and confused their words? The purpose of fasting is not hunger and thirst. It is, instead, to discipline and uplift. There are, in fact, more than ten misdeeds that may emanate from the tongue if it is not properly controlled. Among them: lying, backbiting, slander, obscenity, cursing, shamelessness, false evidence, invective, derision, scorn and others. Perhaps a word uttered by someone without any control or restraint may land them on his face in the fire.

The tongue is a means to good or evil. What a delight it would be for those who remember Allah, seek His forgiveness, praise Him, glorify Him, give thanks to Him, and repent with their tongues. And, what a disappointment it would be for those who use it to violate honour and sanctity and besmirch values. O fasting people, moisten your tongue with the remembrance of Allah, discipline it with God-consciousness and cleanse it from disobedience. O Allah we ask of You truthful tongues, pure hearts and upright characters.

Lesson 10

How does the eye fast?

And there is also the fasting of the eye. What kind of fast? The fast of the eye is to prevent it from seeing forbidden things and to cover it from indecencies. 'Tell the believing men to lower their gaze and to be mindful of their chastity; this will be most conducive to their purity – [and,] verily, God is aware of all that they do. And tell the believing women to lower their gaze and to be mindful of their chastity, and not to display their charms [in public] beyond what may [decently] be apparent thereof; hence, let them draw their head-covering over their bosoms' (24:30–31).

قُل لِّلْمُؤْمِنِينَ يَغُضُّوا۟ مِنْ أَبْصَٰرِهِمْ وَيَحْفَظُوا۟ فُرُوجَهُمْ ذَٰلِكَ أَزْكَىٰ لَهُمْ إِنَّ ٱللَّهَ خَبِيرٌۢ بِمَا يَصْنَعُونَ ۝ وَقُل لِّلْمُؤْمِنَٰتِ يَغْضُضْنَ مِنْ أَبْصَٰرِهِنَّ وَيَحْفَظْنَ فُرُوجَهُنَّ وَلَا يُبْدِينَ زِينَتَهُنَّ إِلَّا مَا ظَهَرَ مِنْهَا وَلْيَضْرِبْنَ بِخُمُرِهِنَّ عَلَىٰ جُيُوبِهِنَّ وَلَا يُبْدِينَ زِينَتَهُنَّ إِلَّا لِبُعُولَتِهِنَّ أَوْ ءَابَآئِهِنَّ أَوْ ءَابَآءِ بُعُولَتِهِنَّ أَوْ أَبْنَآئِهِنَّ أَوْ أَبْنَآءِ بُعُولَتِهِنَّ أَوْ إِخْوَٰنِهِنَّ أَوْ بَنِىٓ إِخْوَٰنِهِنَّ أَوْ بَنِىٓ أَخَوَٰتِهِنَّ أَوْ نِسَآئِهِنَّ أَوْ مَا مَلَكَتْ أَيْمَٰنُهُنَّ أَوِ ٱلتَّٰبِعِينَ غَيْرِ أُو۟لِى ٱلْإِرْبَةِ مِنَ

ٱلرِّجَالِ أَوِ ٱلطِّفْلِ ٱلَّذِينَ لَمْ يَظْهَرُوا۟ عَلَىٰ عَوْرَٰتِ ٱلنِّسَآءِ ۖ وَلَا يَضْرِبْنَ بِأَرْجُلِهِنَّ لِيُعْلَمَ مَا يُخْفِينَ مِن زِينَتِهِنَّ ۚ وَتُوبُوٓا۟ إِلَى ٱللَّهِ جَمِيعًا أَيُّهَ ٱلْمُؤْمِنُونَ لَعَلَّكُمْ تُفْلِحُونَ

The eye is an opening to the heart and a door to the spirit. Ali ibn Abi Talib once asked the Prophet about the gaze. He ﷺ replied: 'Lower your gaze.' Hence whoever does not lower his gaze will be afflicted by four calamities:

1. The disposing of the heart in every direction, and its tearing apart in every field. As a consequence, it has no stability and enjoys no inner peace. Neither is it able to mobilize all its power. It is wounded and weakened and quite rightly complains of the misdeeds of the eyes, its gazes and glances.

2. Punishment of the soul and training it with the loss of what it saw and did not get. The soul, because of the act of the eye, is in constant distress, anxiety and turmoil.

3. With the release of forbidden glances, the sweetness of worship and obedience is lost. Thus, say goodbye to the light of faith if the eye is not disciplined and made to fast from the unlawful sights. The souls will neither taste faith nor find conviction except through the control of the eyes.

4. Because of the great sin incurred by its violation of honour and privacy, the eyes would be rewarded with great sin. No one ever fell into filth and perversion except after his eyes had gone astray. Surely there is no movement and no power except with Allah the most High, the most Magnificent.

One of our righteous forebears said: 'I once looked at something that was forbidden and I forgot the Quran.' After forty years, Allah rewarded him for lowering his gaze by endowing him with faith the sweetness of which he tasted in his heart. Thus it is often said that the eye is the pathfinder. If it is sent out, it hunts. If it is bridled, it follows. And, if it is let loose, it lands the heart in vice. Likewise, others have commented about the eye: 'If its rein gets out of control, it dashes you and if you release its lead, it hurts you.'

Still in addition, Shah al Karmani observed: 'Whoever lowered his gaze from forbidden things and nourished his stomach with the fear of God and displayed it by following the Sunnah of the Prophet, his intuition will never mislead him.' Al Karmani completed this comment with the Quranic verse: 'Verily, in all this there are messages indeed for those who can read the signs' (15:75).

إِنَّ فِى ذَٰلِكَ لَآيَٰتٍ لِّلْمُتَوَسِّمِينَ

There are five benefits and honours to be gained from lowering the gaze:

1.   Obedience to Allah Almighty's command to lower the gaze. This, by itself is enough as a blessing and honour in this world and the next.

2.   Peace of the heart, its nourishment as well as its realization of its full potential, comfort, happiness and ease.

3.   Avoidance of calamities and safety from trials and misdeeds.

4.   Allah opens for His servant the doors of knowledge, understanding, success and uprightness; a fitting reward for his piety.

5.   Allah will instil a sense of discernment in the heart

of the learned and His perfect light in the souls of the truthful; again a reward for those who lowered their gazes.

Accordingly, when Ramadan comes, the eyes are expected to fast in obedience to the Ever Living, the Self-Subsisting. The benefits of hunger are all too many, simply because of the eye. Know, therefore, that hunger curtails the excesses of the eye and restrains its misdeeds and limits their scope. Similarly, hunger weakens the desire to gaze and it stifles the heat of the sight.

When the licentious release their gazes and fill their eyes they fall into the filth of disobedience and the snares of indecency. They are some people whose stomachs fast from food and drink but their eyes graze in the shrubbery of forbidden sights. Such people do not know the real essence of fasting. O servant of Allah, let our eyes fast from the unlawful things in the same way that we abstain from food and drink. Let our hearts be healthy and our spirits relax. 'And so, God will preserve them from the woes of that Day, and will bestow on them brightness and joy, and will reward them for all their patience in adversity with a garden [of bliss] and with [garments of] silk' (76:11–12).

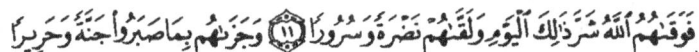

May the peace, mercy and blessings of Allah be upon the one whose eyes fast for the pleasure of his Lord.

Lesson 11

How does the ear fast?

Allah says: 'Verily [thy] hearing and sight and heart – all of them – will be called to account for it [on Judgement Day]!' (17:36).

وَلَا تَقْفُ مَا لَيْسَ لَكَ بِهِ عِلْمٌ إِنَّ ٱلسَّمْعَ وَٱلْبَصَرَ وَٱلْفُؤَادَ كُلُّ أُوْلَٰٓئِكَ كَانَ عَنْهُ مَسْـُٔولًا

The ear is responsible before Allah for what it hears. The righteous people are those who listen carefully to what is said and follow it. And what regret there will be for the one who turned his hearing away from the guidance and closed his eyes from the voice of truth.

The ear fasts from listening to obscenities, music and all forms of lewd material. To the righteous there is an illustrious fast from hearing things that will anger Allah Almighty both in and out of Ramadan. Many people hampered the limbs that Allah bestowed upon them. Allah confirms this in His Quran: 'And most certainly We have destined for hell many of the invisible beings and men who have hearts with which they fail to grasp the truth, and eyes with which they fail to see, and ears with which they fail to hear. They are like cattle – nay, they are even less conscious of the right way: it is they, they who are the [truly] heedless!' (7:179).

وَلَقَدْ ذَرَأْنَا لِجَهَنَّمَ كَثِيرًا مِّنَ ٱلْجِنِّ وَٱلْإِنسِ ۖ لَهُمْ قُلُوبٌ لَّا يَفْقَهُونَ بِهَا وَلَهُمْ أَعْيُنٌ لَّا يُبْصِرُونَ بِهَا وَلَهُمْ ءَاذَانٌ لَّا يَسْمَعُونَ بِهَا ۚ أُوْلَٰٓئِكَ كَٱلْأَنْعَٰمِ بَلْ هُمْ أَضَلُّ ۚ أُوْلَٰٓئِكَ هُمُ ٱلْغَٰفِلُونَ

Yes they have ears but they do not listen, ponder over or understand advice. The hearing of many people is completely like the hearing of the cattle, no remembrance or reflection, no benefit or advantage. Allah says of them: 'Or dost thou think that most of them listen [to thy message] and use their reason? Nay, they are but like cattle – nay, they are even less conscious of the right way!' (25:44).

أَمْ تَحْسَبُ أَنَّ أَكْثَرَهُمْ يَسْمَعُونَ أَوْ يَعْقِلُونَ ۚ إِنْ هُمْ إِلَّا كَٱلْأَنْعَٰمِ ۖ بَلْ هُمْ أَضَلُّ سَبِيلًا

Among the people are those who fill their hearing with forbidden sounds and sinful words. They forbid their ears to listen to the Noble Quran, that lawful, distinctive and divine audition. Listening to the Quran bears the fruit of faith, guidance, light and prosperity. It fills the heart with wisdom, tranquillity, intimacy and contentment. It is a source of protection from the dangerous, deviant and sinful thoughts. Thus, the power of the ears lies in remembrance, beneficial knowledge, good advice, profound manners, remarkable knowledge and good speech.

Abi Hatim reported that he once passed by an old woman in Madinah and heard her reading the Quran from behind her door. She was crying and repeating the verse:

'Has there come unto thee the tidings of the Overshadowing event?' Abi Hatim began to listen and repeat: 'Yes it came to me, yes it came to me.' Allah praises those who perfect the listening to the Quran by pointing out: 'For, when they come to understand what has been bestowed from on high upon this Apostle, thou canst see their eyes overflow with tears, because they recognize something of the truth' (5:83).

وَإِذَا سَمِعُوا مَا أُنزِلَ إِلَى ٱلرَّسُولِ تَرَىٰٓ أَعۡيُنَهُمۡ تَفِيضُ مِنَ ٱلدَّمۡعِ مِمَّا عَرَفُوا۟ مِنَ ٱلۡحَقِّ يَقُولُونَ رَبَّنَآ ءَامَنَّا فَٱكۡتُبۡنَا مَعَ ٱلشَّٰهِدِينَ

They certainly have had the greatest benefit and listened in the best manner. Thus the ears of those who fast are tuned to hear what is beautiful while the ears of the foolish are trained to hear falsehood. If the ears of a Muslim allow sinful words to enter, it would wreck the house of the heart, destroy the palace of volition and corrupt the garden of knowledge.

This is how Allah describes these two groups: 'Yet whenever a *surah* [of this divine writ] is bestowed from on high, some of the deniers of the truth are prone to ask, "Which of you has this [message] strengthened in his faith?" Now as for those who have attained to faith, it does strengthen them in their faith, and they rejoice in the glad tidings [which God has given them]. But as for those in whose hearts is disease, each new message but adds another [element of] disbelief to the disbelief which they already harbour, and they die while [still] refusing to acknowledge the truth' (9:124–5).

وَإِذَا مَآ أُنزِلَتۡ سُورَةٌ فَمِنۡهُم مَّن يَقُولُ أَيُّكُمۡ زَادَتۡهُ هَٰذِهِۦٓ إِيمَٰنٗاۚ فَأَمَّا ٱلَّذِينَ ءَامَنُوا۟ فَزَادَتۡهُمۡ إِيمَٰنٗا وَهُمۡ يَسۡتَبۡشِرُونَ ۝ وَأَمَّا ٱلَّذِينَ فِى قُلُوبِهِم مَّرَضٞ فَزَادَتۡهُمۡ رِجۡسًا إِلَىٰ رِجۡسِهِمۡ وَمَاتُوا۟ وَهُمۡ كَٰفِرُونَ

Listening to the truth increases the heart in steadfastness on the path of truth. And, on the contrary, listening to falsehood leaves traces of falsehood in the heart. It is, therefore, the duty of every Muslim to praise Allah for the blessing of hearing and also to use it to gain the pleasure of his Lord. Toward this end, the Muslim must engage more in the reading of the Quran, studying, and attendance of useful lectures and advanced wisdom.

The Muslim must save his ear from listening to sin, indecency and all that impedes one on the path of Allah. Allah Almighty says concerning his righteous servants that they 'turn away from all that is frivolous' (23:3).

وَٱلَّذِينَ هُمْ عَنِ ٱللَّغْوِ مُعْرِضُونَ

And: 'Whenever they heard frivolous talk, having turned away from it and said: "Unto us shall be accounted our deeds, and unto you, your deeds. Peace be upon you – [but] we do not seek out such as are ignorant [of the meaning of right and wrong]"' (28:55).

وَإِذَا سَمِعُوا ٱللَّغْوَ أَعْرَضُوا عَنْهُ وَقَالُوا لَنَا أَعْمَالُنَا وَلَكُمْ أَعْمَالُكُمْ سَلَامٌ عَلَيْكُمْ لَا نَبْتَغِي ٱلْجَاهِلِينَ

Lesson 12

How does the stomach fast?

Lawful and unlawful food both affect the life, behaviour and character of man. Hence Allah has ordered: 'O you apostles! Partake of the good things of life, and do righteous deeds' (23:51).

$$\text{يَٰٓأَيُّهَا ٱلرُّسُلُ كُلُوا۟ مِنَ ٱلطَّيِّبَٰتِ وَٱعْمَلُوا۟ صَٰلِحًا إِنِّى بِمَا تَعْمَلُونَ عَلِيمٌ}$$

Similarly, He says to the believers: 'O you who have attained faith! Partake of the good things which We have provided for you as sustenance, and render thanks unto God, if it is [truly] Him that you worship' (2:172).

$$\text{يَٰٓأَيُّهَا ٱلَّذِينَ ءَامَنُوا۟ كُلُوا۟ مِن طَيِّبَٰتِ مَا رَزَقْنَٰكُمْ وَٱشْكُرُوا۟ لِلَّهِ إِن كُنتُمْ إِيَّاهُ تَعْبُدُونَ}$$

The good are those things which Allah Almighty has made lawful for His servants through His Prophet ﷺ. He says: '[The Prophet] makes lawful to them the good things of life and forbids them the bad things' (7:157).

$$\text{الَّذِينَ يَتَّبِعُونَ الرَّسُولَ النَّبِيَّ الْأُمِّيَّ الَّذِي يَجِدُونَهُ مَكْتُوبًا عِندَهُمْ فِي التَّوْرَىٰةِ وَالْإِنجِيلِ يَأْمُرُهُم بِالْمَعْرُوفِ وَيَنْهَاهُمْ عَنِ الْمُنكَرِ وَيُحِلُّ لَهُمُ الطَّيِّبَـٰتِ وَيُحَرِّمُ عَلَيْهِمُ الْخَبَـٰٓئِثَ وَيَضَعُ عَنْهُمْ إِصْرَهُمْ وَالْأَغْلَـٰلَ الَّتِي كَانَتْ عَلَيْهِمْ ۚ فَالَّذِينَ ءَامَنُوا بِهِۦ وَعَزَّرُوهُ وَنَصَرُوهُ وَاتَّبَعُوا النُّورَ الَّذِي أُنزِلَ مَعَهُۥٓ ۙ أُو۟لَـٰٓئِكَ هُمُ الْمُفْلِحُونَ}$$

The fasting of the stomach implies its avoidance of unlawful things. Apart from the abstinence from food, drink and all that invalidates the fast during the days of Ramadan, it also requires avoidance of the prohibited things after the breaking of the fast. Thus he does not eat from the proceeds of interest, for if he does so he will earn the anger of his Lord Most High. Allah says: 'O you who attained faith! Do not gorge yourselves on usury, doubling and redoubling it' (3:130).

$$\text{يَـٰٓأَيُّهَا الَّذِينَ ءَامَنُوا لَا تَأْكُلُوا الرِّبَوٰٓا۟ أَضْعَـٰفًا مُّضَـٰعَفَةً ۖ وَاتَّقُوا اللَّهَ لَعَلَّكُمْ تُفْلِحُونَ}$$

And: 'God has made buying and selling lawful and usury unlawful' (2:275).

$$\text{الَّذِينَ يَأْكُلُونَ الرِّبَوٰا۟ لَا يَقُومُونَ إِلَّا كَمَا يَقُومُ الَّذِي يَتَخَبَّطُهُ الشَّيْطَـٰنُ مِنَ الْمَسِّ ۚ ذَٰلِكَ بِأَنَّهُمْ قَالُوٓا۟ إِنَّمَا الْبَيْعُ مِثْلُ الرِّبَوٰا۟ ۗ وَأَحَلَّ اللَّهُ الْبَيْعَ وَحَرَّمَ الرِّبَوٰا۟ ۚ فَمَن جَآءَهُۥ مَوْعِظَةٌ مِّن رَّبِّهِۦ فَانتَهَىٰ فَلَهُۥ مَا سَلَفَ وَأَمْرُهُۥٓ إِلَى اللَّهِ ۖ وَمَنْ عَادَ فَأُو۟لَـٰٓئِكَ أَصْحَـٰبُ النَّارِ ۖ هُمْ فِيهَا خَـٰلِدُونَ}$$

Concerning this matter the Prophet ﷺ declared: 'God has cursed the one who eats the proceeds of interest, the one who gives it, the one who writes it, and the witness thereof; they are all the same.'

In reality, the one who eats from interest is actually fooling himself. For by filling his stomach with unlawful gain, he has effectively closed the doors for the acceptance of his prayers, no matter how much he may call upon Allah. The Prophet ﷺ mentioned to his companions the case of a man who, having journeyed far, is dishevelled and has dusty hair. He spread his hands out to the sky asking his Lord while his food and drink were unlawful, so how can his prayers be answered. This man was, indeed, very religious. He worshipped a great deal. But he sinned concerning his food, not fearing Allah in what he ate or drank.

How can the stomach be considered fasting when it eats from unlawful food gained from the wealth of orphans, interest, cheating and force? Surely by Allah, the taste would be spoiled when the food and drink is contaminated. The hearts would be hardened when the food and drink is filthy. And the light will go out when lawful sustenance is lost. It was reported that Abu Bakr al Siddiq was eating one day when he questioned his servant about the origin of the food. The servant said from soothsaying, a practice he used to engage in prior to Islam. Abu Bakr became angry and vomited all that was in his stomach. Allah thereafter purified and accepted all that he gave in charity.

On the whole, food stays in the stomach of the one who consumed it. Its traces remain with the flesh and blood. Thus any body that is nourished by unlawful food will find its destiny in the fire of hell. The righteous predecessors knew from where they were eating. Their tastes were pure and, as a result, their bodies became healthy and their hearts were enlightened. When the food and drink of their successors were defiled, the signals of guidance in their hearts were extinguished. The Prophet ﷺ said: 'A servant has never eaten better food than what he earned with his hand.' And, that the Prophet David used to eat the food that he earned with his hand. Indeed, while David was a known to be an ironmonger, Zakariya was himself a carpenter and Muhammad ﷺ and the other prophets were shepherds.

Islam thus encourages the seeking and earning of sustenance from lawful means. As Allah says in the Quran: 'And do not touch the substance of an orphan, save to improve it' (17:34).

وَلَا تَقْرَبُوا مَالَ ٱلْيَتِيمِ إِلَّا بِٱلَّتِي هِيَ أَحْسَنُ حَتَّىٰ يَبْلُغَ أَشُدَّهُۥ وَأَوْفُوا بِٱلْعَهْدِ إِنَّ ٱلْعَهْدَ كَانَ مَسْـُٔولًا

And: 'Behold, those who sinfully devour the possessions of orphans but fill their bellies with fire: for [in the life to come] they will have to endure a blazing flame!' (4:10).

إِنَّ ٱلَّذِينَ يَأْكُلُونَ أَمْوَٰلَ ٱلْيَتَٰمَىٰ ظُلْمًا إِنَّمَا يَأْكُلُونَ فِي بُطُونِهِمْ نَارًا وَسَيَصْلَوْنَ سَعِيرًا

'And devour not one another's possessions wrongfully, and neither employ legal artifices with a view to devouring sinfully, and knowingly, anything that by right belongs to others' (2:188).

وَلَا تَأْكُلُوا أَمْوَٰلَكُم بَيْنَكُم بِٱلْبَٰطِلِ وَتُدْلُوا بِهَآ إِلَى ٱلْحُكَّامِ لِتَأْكُلُوا فَرِيقًا مِّنْ أَمْوَٰلِ ٱلنَّاسِ بِٱلْإِثْمِ وَأَنتُمْ تَعْلَمُونَ

'Those who gorge themselves on usury behave but as he might behave whom Satan has confounded with his touch' (2:275).

ٱلَّذِينَ يَأْكُلُونَ ٱلرِّبَوٰا۟ لَا يَقُومُونَ إِلَّا كَمَا يَقُومُ ٱلَّذِى يَتَخَبَّطُهُ ٱلشَّيْطَٰنُ مِنَ ٱلْمَسِّ ذَٰلِكَ بِأَنَّهُمْ قَالُوٓا۟ إِنَّمَا ٱلْبَيْعُ مِثْلُ ٱلرِّبَوٰا۟ وَأَحَلَّ ٱللَّهُ ٱلْبَيْعَ وَحَرَّمَ ٱلرِّبَوٰا۟ فَمَن جَآءَهُۥ مَوْعِظَةٌ مِّن رَّبِّهِۦ فَٱنتَهَىٰ فَلَهُۥ مَا سَلَفَ وَأَمْرُهُۥٓ إِلَى ٱللَّهِ وَمَنْ عَادَ فَأُو۟لَٰٓئِكَ أَصْحَٰبُ ٱلنَّارِ هُمْ فِيهَا خَٰلِدُونَ

In an authentic *hadith*, the Prophet ﷺ said: 'Allah has cursed the one who bribes and the one who accepts bribes.' The Quran itself condemns the corruption of the Christians and the Jews: 'And thou canst see many of them vie with one another in sinning and tyrannical conduct and in their swallowing of all that is evil' (5:62).

وَتَرَىٰ كَثِيرًا مِّنْهُمْ يُسَٰرِعُونَ فِى ٱلْإِثْمِ وَٱلْعُدْوَٰنِ وَأَكْلِهِمُ ٱلسُّحْتَ لَبِئْسَ مَا كَانُوا۟ يَعْمَلُونَ

Ibn al Jawzi narrates in *Sayd al Khatir* that he once ate something that was questionable and his heart changed and became darkened for a period thereafter. Such was the consciousness of our forebears that they felt the changes in their hearts as they strove to purify them. As for many of our folk today, they eat as they like without sensing any changes in their hearts. That is because whoever desires disgrace, the way to accomplish that would be made easy for him. Some of them consume alcohol and other forms of illegal intoxicants, thereby denying themselves the delight of worship and sweetness of obedience. Thus they live submerged in anxiety and forbidden from happiness and an hour when their prayers would be accepted.

O you who fast! Know that there is a fast of the stomach. Who does not observe it, it is as if he did not fast.

Are there not some who would refrain from the unlawful and strictly observe their food and drink in order to enter the Paradise? O Allah, make us among those who sanction the lawful things endorsed by the Islamic Shariah and make us prevent those things which are unlawful.

Lesson 13

Mistakes made by those who fast?

Many of those who fast make mistakes because they do not understand Allah's religion, including matters relating to fasting. They, accordingly, do not know what are the things that invalidate, impair or harm the fast. Neither have they any knowledge of the things they ought do while fasting, what is allowed, what is obligatory and what is forbidden. The Prophet ﷺ said: 'Whoever Allah wishes good, He grants understanding in religion.' Thus, it appears that the one who does not understand or ask about his religion is such a person whom Allah does not wish well.

Additionally, Allah Almighty says: 'And [even] before thy time, [O Muhammad,] We never sent [as Our apostles] any but [mortal] men, whom We inspired: and if you have not [yet] realized this, ask those who possess the message' (16:43).

وَمَآ أَرۡسَلۡنَا مِن قَبۡلِكَ إِلَّا رِجَالًا نُّوحِىٓ إِلَيۡهِمۡ فَسۡـَٔلُوٓاْ أَهۡلَ ٱلذِّكۡرِ إِن كُنتُمۡ لَا تَعۡلَمُونَ

Those who possess the message here are the scholars. Thus

it is only fitting that the Muslim who really wants to worship Allah faithfully should ask about the matters he does not know about his religion. He should, furthermore, seek knowledge and try to understand his faith.

Some people who fast commit great sins that nullify their fast. Foremost among these is backbiting. Some of these, which were mentioned in the lesson of 'How does the tongue fast?' include slander, indecent conversation, derision, swearing and others.

Among the other mistakes is the wasting of money on meals both at the beginning and the breaking of the fast in Ramadan. They prepare food enough for a crowd of people consisting of numerous dishes, cheap and expensive with drinks that are sweet, sour and even salted. Then, at the end of all this, they eat only a little and throw the remainder into the refuse. This, no doubt, is contrary to the great teachings of Islam. Allah Almighty says: 'And eat and drink [freely], but do not waste: verily, He does not love the wasteful!' (7:31).

يَٰبَنِىٓ ءَادَمَ خُذُوا۟ زِينَتَكُمْ عِندَ كُلِّ مَسْجِدٍ وَكُلُوا۟ وَٱشْرَبُوا۟ وَلَا تُسْرِفُوٓا۟ إِنَّهُۥ لَا يُحِبُّ ٱلْمُسْرِفِينَ

Everything that exceeds man's needs is considered an abominable waste. Allah the Lord of those who fast does not like extravagance. This is illustrated in His words: 'Do not squander [thy substance] senselessly. Behold, the squanderers are, indeed, of the ilk of the satans – in as much as Satan has indeed proved most ungrateful to his Sustainer' (17:26–7).

وَءَاتِ ذَا ٱلْقُرْبَىٰ حَقَّهُۥ وَٱلْمِسْكِينَ وَٱبْنَ ٱلسَّبِيلِ وَلَا تُبَذِّرْ تَبْذِيرًا ﴿٦﴾ إِنَّ ٱلْمُبَذِّرِينَ كَانُوٓا۟ إِخْوَٰنَ ٱلشَّيَٰطِينِ وَكَانَ ٱلشَّيْطَٰنُ لِرَبِّهِۦ كَفُورًا

Likewise He commends: 'Those who, whenever they spend on others, are neither wasteful nor niggardly but [remember that] there is always a just mean between those [two extremes]' (25:67).

وَٱلَّذِينَ إِذَآ أَنفَقُوا۟ لَمْ يُسْرِفُوا۟ وَلَمْ يَقْتُرُوا۟ وَكَانَ بَيْنَ ذَٰلِكَ قَوَامًا

During Ramadan our market places are filled with buyers, all of them carrying enough food and drink to feed tens of families. Yet, there are families dying from hunger because they cannot find a piece of bread. They sleep under the open skies making their beds upon the dirt while families here are afflicted with indigestion caused by their extravagance and showing off. One of the purposes of fasting is to empty the stomach of all contaminated material by reducing the intake of food. But, how can those who indulge in excessive eating and drinking, and waste much more, realize this?

Many people spend their fasting hours sleeping. As a result it seems as if they did not fast. Of these, they are some who only awake to pray and then return to sleep. They, as it were, pass their days in neglect and their nights awake. Neither their long sleep nor their staying up at night will increase or reduce their age. The wisdom of fasting, therefore, is that the one who fasts should experience the pangs of hunger and savour thirst in order to gain the pleasure of Allah. The one who devotes his entire day to sleep will not attain this.

Among the fasting people are those who play games that are, at the very least, regarded as despicable in the Islamic law. They kill their valuable time in futile games which they claim help them to relax. Allah says: 'Did you, then think that We created you in mere idle play, and that you would not have to return to Us?' (23:115).

أَفَحَسِبْتُمْ أَنَّمَا خَلَقْنَٰكُمْ عَبَثًا وَأَنَّكُمْ إِلَيْنَا لَا تُرْجَعُونَ

And: 'Leave to themselves all those who, beguiled by the life of this world, have made play and passing delights their religion' (6:70).

وَذَرِ الَّذِينَ اتَّخَذُوا دِينَهُمْ لَعِبًا وَلَهْوًا وَغَرَّتْهُمُ الْحَيَاةُ الدُّنْيَا وَذَكِّرْ بِهِ أَن تُبْسَلَ نَفْسٌ بِمَا كَسَبَتْ لَيْسَ لَهَا مِن دُونِ اللَّهِ وَلِيٌّ وَلَا شَفِيعٌ وَإِن تَعْدِلْ كُلَّ عَدْلٍ لَّا يُؤْخَذْ مِنْهَا ۗ أُولَٰئِكَ الَّذِينَ أُبْسِلُوا بِمَا كَسَبُوا ۖ لَهُمْ شَرَابٌ مِّنْ حَمِيمٍ وَعَذَابٌ أَلِيمٌ بِمَا كَانُوا يَكْفُرُونَ

There are besides other people who fast and spend their entire nights awake in futile activities. They engage in amusement, play and deviance without ever offering a single prayer in the darkness of night. Among the worst mistakes perpetrated by some fasters is their failure to perform collective prayers for the most trifling excuses. This, of course, is among the signs of hypocrisy and evidence of sick hearts and dead spirits.

There are others, still, who have no relationship or closeness with the Quran during Ramadan. They read much, but not the Glorious Quran. They delve into many books but not the book of Allah the Most High.

It is certainly regrettable that during the great month of Ramadan there are also people who make no effort to do good for themselves by giving charity. They do not honour their tables by allowing others to break their fast with them. Their doors are shut and their fists are tight. Allah says to them: 'All that is with you is bound to come to an end, whereas that which is with God is everlasting' (16:96).

مَا عِندَكُمْ يَنفَدُ ۖ وَمَا عِندَ اللَّهِ بَاقٍ ۗ وَلَنَجْزِيَنَّ الَّذِينَ صَبَرُوا أَجْرَهُم بِأَحْسَنِ مَا كَانُوا يَعْمَلُونَ

And: 'For whatever good deed you may offer up in your own behalf, you shall truly find it with God – yea, better, and richer in reward' (73:20).

إِنَّ رَبَّكَ يَعْلَمُ أَنَّكَ تَقُومُ أَدْنَىٰ مِن ثُلُثَىِ ٱلَّيْلِ وَنِصْفَهُۥ وَثُلُثَهُۥ وَطَآئِفَةٌ مِّنَ ٱلَّذِينَ مَعَكَ وَٱللَّهُ يُقَدِّرُ ٱلَّيْلَ وَٱلنَّهَارَ عَلِمَ أَن لَّن تُحْصُوهُ فَتَابَ عَلَيْكُمْ فَٱقْرَءُوا۟ مَا تَيَسَّرَ مِنَ ٱلْقُرْءَانِ عَلِمَ أَن سَيَكُونُ مِنكُم مَّرْضَىٰ وَءَاخَرُونَ يَضْرِبُونَ فِى ٱلْأَرْضِ يَبْتَغُونَ مِن فَضْلِ ٱللَّهِ وَءَاخَرُونَ يُقَٰتِلُونَ فِى سَبِيلِ ٱللَّهِ فَٱقْرَءُوا۟ مَا تَيَسَّرَ مِنْهُ وَأَقِيمُوا۟ ٱلصَّلَوٰةَ وَءَاتُوا۟ ٱلزَّكَوٰةَ وَأَقْرِضُوا۟ ٱللَّهَ قَرْضًا حَسَنًا وَمَا تُقَدِّمُوا۟ لِأَنفُسِكُم مِّنْ خَيْرٍ تَجِدُوهُ عِندَ ٱللَّهِ هُوَ خَيْرًا وَأَعْظَمَ أَجْرًا وَٱسْتَغْفِرُوا۟ ٱللَّهَ إِنَّ ٱللَّهَ غَفُورٌ رَّحِيمٌ

Apart from the categories already cited, there are besides some people who forsake the *Taraweeh* prayer in Ramadan and ignore it completely. Such individuals are apparently driven by their inner voices that tell them their performance of the compulsory prayers is enough. These same persons are, however, never satisfied with a little of this world. They seek by all means its non-essentials as well as its necessities. And if you come individually on the Day of the Gathering and you see the different stations in it. On that Day regret will be immense because of the loss of what you wasted in this worldly life.

And finally, there remain another group who fast and yet inconvenience their families with the responsibility of making so much food and drink that they are left with very little time for the Quran, Prophetic traditions, remembrance of Allah and worship. If their demands were limited to the necessities, their families would surely find greater time to expend in the worship of Allah Almighty.

O Allah! Increase us and do not decrease us. Bestow upon us and do not deny us. Honour us and do not disgrace us. Pardon us and grant us forgiveness.

Lesson 14

Our Memories in Ramadan

The most beautiful memory we Muslims have in the month of Ramadan is that our great book and wise reminder was revealed in this month. Allah says; 'It was the month of Ramadan in which the Quran was [first] bestowed from on high as a guidance unto man and a self-evident proof of that guidance, and as the standard by which to discern the true from the false' (2:185).

شَهْرُ رَمَضَانَ ٱلَّذِىٓ أُنزِلَ فِيهِ ٱلْقُرْءَانُ هُدًى لِّلنَّاسِ وَبَيِّنَٰتٍ مِّنَ ٱلْهُدَىٰ وَٱلْفُرْقَانِ فَمَن شَهِدَ مِنكُمُ ٱلشَّهْرَ فَلْيَصُمْهُ وَمَن كَانَ مَرِيضًا أَوْ عَلَىٰ سَفَرٍ فَعِدَّةٌ مِّنْ أَيَّامٍ أُخَرَ يُرِيدُ ٱللَّهُ بِكُمُ ٱلْيُسْرَ وَلَا يُرِيدُ بِكُمُ ٱلْعُسْرَ وَلِتُكْمِلُوا۟ ٱلْعِدَّةَ وَلِتُكَبِّرُوا۟ ٱللَّهَ عَلَىٰ مَا هَدَىٰكُمْ وَلَعَلَّكُمْ تَشْكُرُونَ

Thus the descent of the Quran in Ramadan has made its memory the sweetest of memories and its days the most eternal of all ages.

The Quran was sent down to an unlettered nation to lift them out, by the permission of Allah, of darkness to light. Every time Ramadan comes around it reminds us of this magnificent favour of the revelation of the Quran to the noble Prophet ﷺ. 'No falsehood can ever attain to it openly, and neither in a stealthy manner, [since it is] bestowed from on high by One who is truly wise, ever to be praised' (41:43).

مَا يُقَالُ لَكَ إِلَّا مَا قَدْ قِيلَ لِلرُّسُلِ مِن قَبْلِكَ إِنَّ رَبَّكَ لَذُو مَغْفِرَةٍ وَذُو عِقَابٍ أَلِيمٍ

In Ramadan, we were successful. With the permission of Allah we annihilated disbelief in the Great Battle of Badr. It was a truly a great victory for the Prophet ﷺ and his companions of *Muhajirun* and *Ansars*. 'For, indeed, God did succour you at Badr, when you were utterly weak. Remain, then, conscious of God, so that you might have cause to be grateful' (3:123).

وَلَقَدْ نَصَرَكُمُ اللَّهُ بِبَدْرٍ وَأَنتُمْ أَذِلَّةٌ فَاتَّقُوا اللَّهَ لَعَلَّكُمْ تَشْكُرُونَ

Islam prevailed over disbelief in Ramadan. The banner of 'There is no God save Allah and Muhammad is His Prophet' was raised sublimely in Ramadan, 'On the day when the two forces met in battle' (3:155).

إِنَّ الَّذِينَ تَوَلَّوْا مِنكُمْ يَوْمَ الْتَقَى الْجَمْعَانِ إِنَّمَا اسْتَزَلَّهُمُ الشَّيْطَانُ بِبَعْضِ مَا كَسَبُوا وَلَقَدْ عَفَا اللَّهُ عَنْهُمْ إِنَّ اللَّهَ غَفُورٌ حَلِيمٌ

The Battle of Badr was on the seventeenth of Ramadan; hence every time this day comes around it reminds us of that glorious battle.

The Battle of the Conquest of Makkah also took place in Ramadan. The Quran celebrates the event thus: 'Verily, [O Muhammad,] We have laid open before thee a manifest victory' (48:1).

إِنَّا فَتَحْنَا لَكَ فَتْحًا مُبِينًا

Our Prophet ﷺ conquered hearts in Ramadan, and conquered Makkah with monotheism in Ramadan. The two conquests merged and faith prevailed. The Quran became supreme and the party of the most compassionate was victorious. The great Islamic battles took place in Ramadan and the eternal victories of the Muslims took place in Ramadan.

Among our cherished memories in Ramadan is that the trusted angel, Gabriel, used to descend upon the Prophet Muhammad ﷺ much during this month, teaching and revising with him the verses of the Quran. Gabriel used to help him memorize the Quran and they reflected together upon its sublime meanings and wisdom. For his part, the Prophet ﷺ used to repeat the book to Gabriel and together they harmonized its recitation. They were, undoubtedly, exalted moments of worship, periods of supreme closeness and noble sittings.

Among our memories in Ramadan is the meeting of the first group of companions for the *Taraweeh* prayer. They used to listen to one imam recite the divine book to them. They often cried after contemplating its meanings and were struck by sheer awe and fear of their Lord. The night extended itself with them and they shortened it by standing in prayer. If you witnessed them, the tears flowed from them and reverence became entrenched in their hearts as they were engaged in standing, bowing and prostrating themselves. The expressions poured out from them, their sighs were moaned and raised to the Lord of the earth and the heavens. During those blessed moments their hearts trembled, their skins became cold with fear, and their eyes became earnest and serious with their tears.

We remember further, that the days of Ramadan are those in which the gates of the gardens are opened while those to the fire are shut and the satans are chained. These are definitely the sweetest memories, when the servant of Allah feels that he is shown mercy in this gracious month. And that the wiles of the satans have been turned away from him. Then, for everyone who fasts this month there are two happy moments. He becomes happy when he breaks his fast and when he meets his Lord Most High. Every time this month returns, this exceptional state of happiness and friendly feelings is also renewed and increased.

Every Ramadan, according to the Prophet Muhammad ﷺ, atones for all the sins that were committed during the previous year. It is a month that bears splendid memories for every Muslim of the day he knew that he was cleansed from sin and wrong-doing.

Ramadan is the month of the poor and indigent. They find in it succour and gifts from the rich. They find sustenance and help from the wealthy. Many of them, therefore, become happy during this month because of what they receive from the generous. The Prophet ﷺ said: 'Verily in Paradise there is a gate called *al Rayan* and only the fasting people enter it. Once they enter, it is closed and no one else passes through it.' The gate of *al Rayan* has a special significance for the servants of the Most Compassionate during Ramadan.

> The month of happiness and generosity has come to you,
>
> So greet it with the most beautiful memories

O season of forgiveness embrace us
You are the patron, O time of righteousness.

O Allah grant us the return of many
days of Ramadan over many years,
in garments of righteousness and renewed
repentance.

Lesson 15

Ramadan: the way for Repentance

Perhaps the greatest benefit that accrues to the Muslim in this blessed month is his repentance, his return to Allah, and his evaluation of self and personal history. The door of repentance is open, the grace of your Lord is guaranteed, His favour comes and goes; but where are those who repent and seek forgiveness? Allah advises: 'Say: "O you servants of Mine who have transgressed against your own selves! Despair not of God's mercy: behold, God forgives all sins – for, verily, He alone is much-forgiving, a dispenser of grace!" (39:53).

قُلْ يَٰعِبَادِىَ ٱلَّذِينَ أَسْرَفُوا۟ عَلَىٰٓ أَنفُسِهِمْ لَا تَقْنَطُوا۟ مِن رَّحْمَةِ ٱللَّهِ إِنَّ ٱللَّهَ يَغْفِرُ ٱلذُّنُوبَ جَمِيعًا إِنَّهُۥ هُوَ ٱلْغَفُورُ ٱلرَّحِيمُ

This month, Ramadan, is the season of repentance and forgiveness. It is the month of tolerance and clemency. It is the most precious and cherished of all times. The Prophet ﷺ said: 'Behold, Allah opens His hands at nights to pardon the sinners of the day. And He opens His hands in the day to pardon the transgressors of the night until the sun rises in the west.' Surely our sins are many; yet His compassion is even more. Our misdeeds are great but His mercy is greater. The mistakes we commit are huge; yet his forgiveness is bigger. Glory be to the One who gives while we always do wrong, and continues to do so whatever the errors of the servant. He gives to the one who errs and He does not deny him. His sublimity enables Him to forgive even the one who does wrong.

He says in the Quran: 'And who, when they have committed a shameful deed or have [otherwise] sinned against themselves, remembers God and prays that their sins be forgiven – for who but God could forgive sins? – and does not knowingly persist in doing whatever [wrong] that may have done' (3:135).

وَٱلَّذِينَ إِذَا فَعَلُوا۟ فَٰحِشَةً أَوْ ظَلَمُوٓا۟ أَنفُسَهُمْ ذَكَرُوا۟ ٱللَّهَ فَٱسْتَغْفَرُوا۟ لِذُنُوبِهِمْ وَمَن يَغْفِرُ ٱلذُّنُوبَ إِلَّا ٱللَّهُ وَلَمْ يُصِرُّوا۟ عَلَىٰ مَا فَعَلُوا۟ وَهُمْ يَعْلَمُونَ

They do not ever persist. They make mistakes and acknowledge that they have wronged. They sin and seek forgiveness. They transgress and regret. On account of all this, Allah pardons them. The Prophet ﷺ said: 'What a loss it would be for one to witness Ramadan and not gain from its forgiveness.' It is a rare opportunity. Will you not then strive for its bounties?

Those who are sincere with Allah will find that all their sins throughout the year will be forgiven in Ramadan, if they avoid major sins. The shortcomings and the faults of the entire year are rectified in Ramadan. In a *hadith* Qudsi: 'O My servants, you sin night and day and I forgive all sins; seek My forgiveness and I will forgive you.' Of course it is natural to sin. There are, however, some of us who do not repent, who do not turn to Allah and seek His forgiveness. There are, indeed, some of us who persist in doing wrong. They are the ones who are forsaken and denied guidance along Allah's path. Thus Allah proclaims in a *hadith* Qudsi: 'O son of Adam, you called upon Me and asked of Me; hence I shall forgive you and I will not be inconvenienced.'

O fasting people, this month is our opportunity for sincere repentance. These days are booty for us. Will we not then accept this prize and special opportunity? Take the initiative with sincere repentance before your spirit is taken away. Do not take lightly any sin because your final deeds will also be judged. Many people fasted with us last year and have since departed to their Lord. Does not the authority belong to Him? And, is He not the swiftest of those who judge? Yes, they all went with their deeds and left behind their traces.

Allah says: 'It is He who accepts repentance from His servants, and pardons bad deeds, and knows all that you do' (42:25).

وَهُوَ ٱلَّذِى يَقْبَلُ ٱلتَّوْبَةَ عَنْ عِبَادِهِۦ وَيَعْفُوا۟ عَنِ ٱلسَّيِّـَٔاتِ وَيَعْلَمُ مَا تَفْعَلُونَ

Additionally, the Prophet ﷺ said: 'By the One in whose hands is my soul, if ever you did not sin, Allah would have done away with you and brought another people who would sin and seek His forgiveness. Then He will forgive them.'

And, when will they repent if they fail to do so in Ramadan? When will they return to Allah if they do not return in Ramadan? There are some Muslims who fast in Ramadan, rectify their lives and attain peace of mind. Then, as soon as the blessed month is finished and the fasting is over, they return to their old ways and undermine what was repaired in Ramadan. They breach the covenants they took in Ramadan. Their entire lives are thus spent in building and destroying or pledging and betraying. Allah Almighty warns: 'Hence, be not like her who breaks and completely untwists the yarn which she [herself] has spun and made strong' (16:92).

$$\text{وَلَا تَكُونُوا۟ كَٱلَّتِى نَقَضَتْ غَزْلَهَا مِنۢ بَعْدِ قُوَّةٍ أَنكَٰثًا تَتَّخِذُونَ أَيْمَٰنَكُمْ دَخَلًۢا بَيْنَكُمْ أَن تَكُونَ أُمَّةٌ هِىَ أَرْبَىٰ مِنْ أُمَّةٍ ۚ إِنَّمَا يَبْلُوكُمُ ٱللَّهُ بِهِۦ ۚ وَلَيُبَيِّنَنَّ لَكُمْ يَوْمَ ٱلْقِيَٰمَةِ مَا كُنتُمْ فِيهِ تَخْتَلِفُونَ}$$

When Ramadan ended, many of our predecessors used to cry with its passing. They felt sorry and regretted its departure. That was because of the great progress they achieved, the purification of their hearts, and the illumination of their souls. O Allah, grant us what you granted to our righteous predecessors. Guide us to the straight path.

Lesson 16

Faith increases in Ramadan

Faith increases and decreases according to one's deeds. It increases with obedience and decreases with disobedience. It increases with prayers and uprightness and decreases with corruption and deviance. 'As for those who are [willing to be] guided, He increases their [ability to follow His] guidance and causes them to grow in God-consciousness' (47:17).

وَٱلَّذِينَ ٱهْتَدَوْا زَادَهُمْ هُدًى وَءَاتَىٰهُمْ تَقْوَىٰهُمْ

Allah Almighty also says: 'It is He who from on high has bestowed inner peace upon the hearts of the believers, so that – seeing that God's are all the forces of the heavens and the earth, and that God is all-knowing, truly wise – they might grow yet more firm in their faith' (48:4).

هُوَ ٱلَّذِىٓ أَنزَلَ ٱلسَّكِينَةَ فِى قُلُوبِ ٱلْمُؤْمِنِينَ لِيَزْدَادُوٓا إِيمَٰنًا مَّعَ إِيمَٰنِهِمْ وَلِلَّهِ جُنُودُ ٱلسَّمَٰوَٰتِ وَٱلْأَرْضِ وَكَانَ ٱللَّهُ عَلِيمًا حَكِيمًا

In Ramadan faith increases, conviction grows and monotheism becomes resplendent because of the closeness of the servant to his Lord. Fasting is one of the most righteous deeds and it brings about closeness to Allah. Moreover, it nurtures a special relationship with Allah that distances the Muslim from the fire and from disobedience as well. The standing in Ramadan entails closeness, love, obedience and a yearning to expel hypocrisy from within the Muslim. It also nourishes the tree of faith until it becomes firm and entrenched, producing its fruits all the time with the permission of its Lord.

Here are some of the things that will increase your faith and strengthen your conviction: the performance of congregational prayer with reverence, humility, reflection and attentiveness. 'Verily, for all believers prayer is indeed a sacred duty linked to particular times [of day]' (4:103).

فَإِذَا قَضَيْتُمُ ٱلصَّلَوٰةَ فَٱذْكُرُوا۟ ٱللَّهَ قِيَٰمًا وَقُعُودًا وَعَلَىٰ جُنُوبِكُمْ فَإِذَا ٱطْمَأْنَنتُمْ فَأَقِيمُوا۟ ٱلصَّلَوٰةَ إِنَّ ٱلصَّلَوٰةَ كَانَتْ عَلَى ٱلْمُؤْمِنِينَ كِتَٰبًا مَّوْقُوتًا

Congregational prayer dispels hypocrisy and cultivates piety. Still besides, it prevents indecency and wrong-doing. Allah says in the Quran: 'Prayer restrains man from loathsome deeds and from all that runs counter to reason; and remembrance of God is indeed the greatest [good]. And God knows all that you do' (29:45).

ٱتْلُ مَآ أُوحِىَ إِلَيْكَ مِنَ ٱلْكِتَٰبِ وَأَقِمِ ٱلصَّلَوٰةَ إِنَّ ٱلصَّلَوٰةَ تَنْهَىٰ عَنِ ٱلْفَحْشَآءِ وَٱلْمُنكَرِ وَلَذِكْرُ ٱللَّهِ أَكْبَرُ وَٱللَّهُ يَعْلَمُ مَا تَصْنَعُونَ

The reading of the Quran, reflection upon its verses, living in its shade, breathing its fresh air and following its guidance all serve to increase faith. '[All this We have expounded in this] blessed divine writ which We have revealed unto thee, [O Muhammad,] so that men may ponder over its messages, and so that those who are endowed with insight may take them to heart' (38:29).

$$\text{كِتَٰبٌ أَنزَلْنَٰهُ إِلَيْكَ مُبَٰرَكٌ لِّيَدَّبَّرُوٓاْ ءَايَٰتِهِۦ وَلِيَتَذَكَّرَ أُوْلُواْ ٱلْأَلْبَٰبِ}$$

The fervent and constant remembrance of Allah with the heart, tongue and limbs, with praise and exaltation, all help to increase faith. Remember Him and he will remember you. Call upon Him in the early hours of the morning and seek earnestly His forgiveness.

Seek useful knowledge and understanding of your religion. 'Always say: "O my Sustainer, cause me to grow in knowledge!"' (20:114).

$$\text{فَتَعَٰلَى ٱللَّهُ ٱلْمَلِكُ ٱلْحَقُّ وَلَا تَعْجَلْ بِٱلْقُرْءَانِ مِن قَبْلِ أَن يُقْضَىٰٓ إِلَيْكَ وَحْيُهُۥ وَقُل رَّبِّ زِدْنِي عِلْمًا}$$

Question the people of knowledge. 'And if you have not yet realized this, ask the followers of [earlier] revelation' (16:44).

$$\text{بِٱلْبَيِّنَٰتِ وَٱلزُّبُرِ وَأَنزَلْنَآ إِلَيْكَ ٱلذِّكْرَ لِتُبَيِّنَ لِلنَّاسِ مَا نُزِّلَ إِلَيْهِمْ وَلَعَلَّهُمْ يَتَفَكَّرُونَ}$$

Attend the sittings of remembrance. No one is irritated from sitting with such people. Surely the seeking of knowledge increases faith and reinforces the roots of monotheism. 'Know, then, [O man,] that there is no deity save God, and [while there is yet time,] ask forgiveness for thy sins' (47:19).

$$\text{فَاعْلَمْ أَنَّهُ لَا إِلَهَ إِلَّا اللَّهُ وَاسْتَغْفِرْ لِذَنبِكَ وَلِلْمُؤْمِنِينَ وَالْمُؤْمِنَاتِ وَاللَّهُ يَعْلَمُ مُتَقَلَّبَكُمْ وَمَثْوَاكُمْ}$$

Note, dear reader, that Allah begins this directive here with knowledge before words and deeds.

Charity is yet another factor that increases faith. Although this was discussed in a separate lesson it is important to recognize here that giving and sacrificing raises the station of the servant and purifies him. It disciplines his character and straightens his crooked ways.

Contemplation of the signs of Allah, the Creator, also increases faith. Every Muslim should examine His skilful creation of the universe. The Quran affirms that in the creation and the succession of night and day there are messages for people of insight, those 'who remember God when they stand, and when they sit, and when they lie down to sleep, and [thus] reflect on the creation of the heavens and the earth: "O our Sustainer! Thou hast not created [aught of] this without meaning and purpose. Limitless art Thou in Thy glory! Keep us safe, then, from suffering through fire!"' (3:191).

$$\text{الَّذِينَ يَذْكُرُونَ اللَّهَ قِيَامًا وَقُعُودًا وَعَلَىٰ جُنُوبِهِمْ وَيَتَفَكَّرُونَ فِي خَلْقِ السَّمَاوَاتِ وَالْأَرْضِ رَبَّنَا مَا خَلَقْتَ هَذَا بَاطِلًا سُبْحَانَكَ فَقِنَا عَذَابَ النَّارِ}$$

Ramadan is a time of purification for the reflective mind and illumination of its thoughts. It is a period when discerning hearts are also lighted. It is, therefore, befitting that people of faith should use this occasion to meditate upon the excellent work of the Creator; blessed be His names. For faith decreases, suffers ill health and can, indeed, die. Faith decreases when people abandon the Quran and Sunnah and seek thereafter satisfaction in the junk that comes from human minds. It vanishes when they become obsessed with the mental produce of weak and helpless creatures. Thus if a servant adopts this course he does, in effect, exchange what is good with that which is nearer. By so doing he would have completed his loss and confirmed his destruction. Satan would most certainly overwhelm him. 'Such as these are Satan's partisans: oh, verily, it is they, the partisans of Satan, who will truly be the losers!' (58:19).

$$\text{اسْتَحْوَذَ عَلَيْهِمُ الشَّيْطَانُ فَأَنسَاهُمْ ذِكْرَ اللَّهِ أُوْلَئِكَ حِزْبُ الشَّيْطَانِ أَلَا إِنَّ حِزْبَ الشَّيْطَانِ هُمُ الْخَاسِرُونَ}$$

Amusement, play and association with the people of falsehood similarly cause a decrease of faith. This is usually the fate of those who reject the divine Shari'ah laws and instead choose to wallow in the mire of vice and sensual delights. Allah Almighty warns: 'And pay no heed to any whose heart We have rendered heedless of all remembrance of Us because he had always followed [only] his own desires, abandoning all that is good and true' (18:28).

$$\text{وَاصْبِرْ نَفْسَكَ مَعَ الَّذِينَ يَدْعُونَ رَبَّهُم بِالْغَدَاةِ وَالْعَشِيِّ يُرِيدُونَ وَجْهَهُ وَلَا تَعْدُ عَيْنَاكَ عَنْهُمْ تُرِيدُ زِينَةَ الْحَيَاةِ الدُّنْيَا وَلَا تُطِعْ مَنْ أَغْفَلْنَا قَلْبَهُ عَن ذِكْرِنَا وَاتَّبَعَ هَوَاهُ وَكَانَ أَمْرُهُ فُرُطًا}$$

Other common acts that similarly diminish faith include setting free the limbs in acts of disobedience, defiling parts of the body with misdeeds and blackening the heart with sin. Here, the eye gazes at the unlawful, the ear listens to obscenity, the heart grazes in the fields of carnal desires, the hand oppresses, the sexual organs engage in perversion and the stomach is filled with sin. O Allah! We seek your compassion and mercy. O you who fast and have chastened your limbs from indecency, rejoice with the pleasure of God. Mercy, forgiveness and an abode in Paradise to be inhabited by those who entered through the *al Rayan* gate.

Those who fast must, therefore, ask themselves whether their faith was increased or decreased during Ramadan. Did their conviction become stronger or weaker? For it is only then that they will distinguish between progress and regression and gain from loss.

O Allah! Increase us in faith, conviction, understanding and success.

Lesson 17

The love of Allah becomes greater in Ramadan

Compliance with Allah's command to fast in the month of Ramadan increases the love of Allah in the heart of the one who fasts. The friends of Allah love Him immensely (He loves them and they love Him). There is nothing strange about Allah's expression (they love Him). What is remarkable, however, is His affirmation that [He loves them]. He created them, sustained them, pardoned them and then he loves them.

There are ten signs that indicate love for Allah. Whoever does them has loved Him in deed and not only in word.

1. To love the word that he speaks with and which He revealed to His Prophet ﷺ. To yearn to recite this word and reflect upon its meaning and enjoy closeness to it. To reform the heart with its teachings, let the eyes roam in its gardens, stay awake in the darkness of night with it, act

according to its dictates, and govern with it in every affair of life.

2. To love the Prophet Muhammad ﷺ, follow him and send much praise and blessings upon him. Belief in the Prophet's goodness and acceptance of him as a model. 'Verily, in the Apostle of God you have a good example for everyone who looks forward [with hope and awe] to God and the Last Day, and remembers God unceasingly' (33:21).

لَقَدْ كَانَ لَكُمْ فِى رَسُولِ ٱللَّهِ أُسْوَةٌ حَسَنَةٌ لِّمَن كَانَ يَرْجُواْ ٱللَّهَ وَٱلْيَوْمَ ٱلْءَاخِرَ وَذَكَرَ ٱللَّهَ كَثِيرًا

Acting in accord with his traditions without any reservation, fear or wavering is yet another way of demonstrating one's love for Allah. 'But nay, by they Sustainer! They do not [really] believe unless they make thee [O Prophet] a judge of all on which they disagree among themselves, and then find in their hearts no bar to an acceptance of thy decision and give themselves up [to it] in utter self-surrender' (4:65).

فَلَا وَرَبِّكَ لَا يُؤْمِنُونَ حَتَّىٰ يُحَكِّمُوكَ فِيمَا شَجَرَ بَيْنَهُمْ ثُمَّ لَا يَجِدُواْ فِىٓ أَنفُسِهِمْ حَرَجًا مِّمَّا قَضَيْتَ وَيُسَلِّمُواْ تَسْلِيمًا

3. To jealously guard the limits set down by Allah. And to deter any attempt of transgression against the boundaries of Allah. To feel angry when any of the rites of Islam are dishonoured. To feel pain and anguish because of the condition of this religion among the people of innovation. To strive with heart, tongue and hand as much as possible to uplift Allah's law and establish His religion on earth.

4. To recognize the honour of being a friend of Allah and to strive earnestly to attain that friendship. Allah

describes His friends thus: 'O, verily, they who are close to God – no fear need they have, and neither shall they grieve: They who have attained to faith and have always been conscious of Him.' (10:62)

أَلَا إِنَّ أَوْلِيَاءَ اللَّهِ لَا خَوْفٌ عَلَيْهِمْ وَلَا هُمْ يَحْزَنُونَ

And: 'Behold, your only helper shall be God, and His Apostle, and those who have attained to faith – those that are constant in prayer, and render the purifying dues, and bow down [before God]: for, all who ally themselves with God and His Apostle and those who have attained to faith – behold, it is they, the partisans of God, who shall be victorious!' (5:55–6).

إِنَّمَا وَلِيُّكُمُ اللَّهُ وَرَسُولُهُ وَالَّذِينَ آمَنُوا الَّذِينَ يُقِيمُونَ الصَّلَوٰةَ وَيُؤْتُونَ الزَّكَوٰةَ وَهُمْ رَاكِعُونَ ۝ وَمَن يَتَوَلَّ اللَّهَ وَرَسُولَهُ وَالَّذِينَ آمَنُوا فَإِنَّ حِزْبَ اللَّهِ هُمُ الْغَالِبُونَ

5. To enjoin the right and forbid the wrong and make every valuable sacrifice toward this end. It is the pivot of Islam, its fortification and shield by which it is protected. 'That there might grow out of you a community [of people] who invite unto all that is good, and enjoin the doing of what is right and forbid the doing of what is wrong: and it is they, they who shall attain to a happy state!' (3:104).

وَلْتَكُن مِّنكُمْ أُمَّةٌ يَدْعُونَ إِلَى الْخَيْرِ وَيَأْمُرُونَ بِالْمَعْرُوفِ وَيَنْهَوْنَ عَنِ الْمُنكَرِ ۚ وَأُولَٰئِكَ هُمُ الْمُفْلِحُونَ

This feature is increased in brilliance during the month of Ramadan. The truthful fasters expend their energies in giving advice and calling the servants of Allah. As a result, they gain a great reward from their Lord Most High.

6. To sit with the righteous, love them and enjoy the pleasure of their company. Of the friends of Allah, to listen to their conversations and long to meet and visit them; to say prayers for them and protect their honour; to mention their good qualities and benefit as much as possible from them. For Allah says: 'All believers are but brethren' (49:10).

إِنَّمَا ٱلْمُؤْمِنُونَ إِخْوَةٌ فَأَصْلِحُوا بَيْنَ أَخَوَيْكُمْ وَٱتَّقُوا ٱللَّهَ لَعَلَّكُمْ تُرْحَمُونَ

'And hold fast, all together, unto the bond with God, and do not draw apart from one another' (3:103).

وَٱعْتَصِمُوا بِحَبْلِ ٱللَّهِ جَمِيعًا وَلَا تَفَرَّقُوا وَٱذْكُرُوا نِعْمَتَ ٱللَّهِ عَلَيْكُمْ إِذْ كُنتُمْ أَعْدَاءً فَأَلَّفَ بَيْنَ قُلُوبِكُمْ فَأَصْبَحْتُم بِنِعْمَتِهِ إِخْوَانًا وَكُنتُمْ عَلَىٰ شَفَا حُفْرَةٍ مِّنَ ٱلنَّارِ فَأَنقَذَكُم مِّنْهَا كَذَٰلِكَ يُبَيِّنُ ٱللَّهُ لَكُمْ ءَايَٰتِهِۦ لَعَلَّكُمْ تَهْتَدُونَ

7. To draw closer to Allah with voluntary acts of worship in order to gain the pleasure of Allah. This can be done through righteous acts like, prayers, fasting, charity, pilgrimage (greater and lesser), recitation, remembrance and other similar acts. Allah says: '[And,] verily, they would vie with one another in doing good works, and would call unto Us in yearning and awe; and they were always humble before Us' (21:90).

فَٱسْتَجَبْنَا لَهُۥ وَوَهَبْنَا لَهُۥ يَحْيَىٰ وَأَصْلَحْنَا لَهُۥ زَوْجَهُۥٓ إِنَّهُمْ كَانُوا۟ يُسَٰرِعُونَ فِى ٱلْخَيْرَٰتِ وَيَدْعُونَنَا رَغَبًا وَرَهَبًا وَكَانُوا۟ لَنَا خَٰشِعِينَ

He also says in a *hadith* Qudsi: 'My servant continues to draw near to Me with voluntary works so that I shall love him.'

8. To prefer the eternity of the Hereafter to the transience of this world. And, to prepare for the inevitable departure from this world and meeting with Allah Almighty. Prepare for what is inevitable, as death is destined for the servants. Will you be pleased to be the companion of a people who have provisions and you have none?

9. Sincere repentance and abandonment of disobedience and infractions. Avoid the frivolous and playful from among the people of deviance and immorality. Sitting in their company always causes outbursts of anger, deadly poisoning and persistent disease. Allah says: 'On that day, [erstwhile] friends will be foes unto one another – [all] save the God-conscious' (43:67).

ٱلۡأَخِلَّآءُ يَوۡمَئِذٍۭ بَعۡضُهُمۡ لِبَعۡضٍ عَدُوٌّ إِلَّا ٱلۡمُتَّقِينَ

In this same regard Prophet Muhammad ﷺ said: 'People will be raised on the Day of Judgement with those that they love.'

10. To aspire to martyrdom in the way of Allah and look forward to that day when the soul will be presented solely for the sake of Allah; when the self, wealth and sons would all be sold without seeking from this great sale any profitable arrangement.

'Behold, God has bought of the believers their lives and their possessions, promising them Paradise in return, [and so] they fight in God's cause, and slay, and are slain' (9:111).

وَإِذَا مَآ أُنزِلَتۡ سُورَةٌ فَمِنۡهُم مَّن يَقُولُ أَيُّكُمۡ زَادَتۡهُ هَٰذِهِۦٓ إِيمَٰنٗاۚ فَأَمَّا ٱلَّذِينَ ءَامَنُواْ فَزَادَتۡهُمۡ إِيمَٰنٗا وَهُمۡ يَسۡتَبۡشِرُونَ ۝ وَأَمَّا ٱلَّذِينَ فِى قُلُوبِهِم مَّرَضٞ فَزَادَتۡهُمۡ رِجۡسًا إِلَىٰ رِجۡسِهِمۡ وَمَاتُواْ وَهُمۡ كَٰفِرُونَ

O Allah! Increase us in love for you, in desire for what is with You and in resort to You in repentance. Surely You have power over all things.

Lesson 18

How do we train our children during Ramadan and at other times?

In Ramadan, truthful training becomes manifest. So too does wise guidance in supervising the children. For they are a trust and a charge. The righteous forebears used to train their children to fast and help them to become accustomed to standing in prayer at night. O you who fast and desire that your young ones should succeed with you, here are some matters that would help you to make good the training of your children.

First: Be, O father, an example in your character, behaviour and in your life. Remember that your children look upon you as a father, teacher, guide and model. Allah Almighty says concerning the Prophet Zakariya: ' And so We responded unto him, and bestowed upon him the gift of John, having made his wife fit to bear him a child: [and,] verily, these [three] would vie with one another in doing good works, and would call unto Us in yearning and awe; and they were always humble before Us' (21:90).

$$\text{فَٱسْتَجَبْنَا لَهُ وَوَهَبْنَا لَهُ يَحْيَىٰ وَأَصْلَحْنَا لَهُ زَوْجَهُۥٓ إِنَّهُمْ كَانُوا۟ يُسَٰرِعُونَ فِى ٱلْخَيْرَٰتِ وَيَدْعُونَنَا رَغَبًا وَرَهَبًا وَكَانُوا۟ لَنَا خَٰشِعِينَ}$$

Second: Whatever children see or hear at home has a tremendous impact upon their lives and future. The presence of faith, the Quran and Prophetic traditions in the home, together with much remembrance and enjoining of Allah's commands and avoidance of His prohibitions, all will help in making the child upright and steadfast. The introduction of amusements, enticements, instruments of fun and negligence of Allah's law, all render your child ineffectual, playful and marginal.

Third: Bond the child to Allah's book through memorization and recitation according to its rules of intonation. This is the period of memorization and reception. If the child loses this golden opportunity by wasting it aimlessly in television and relaxation, he will certainly regret it immensely in the future. He will deeply regret the wasting of those precious hours.

Fourth: The companionships of your child during his early years and youth are extremely important. They should be prevented from associating with the vile, corrupt and debased people. They are more harmful to your children than scabies. They can do more damage than any enemy. Only Allah, the God besides whom there is none, knows how many good children these miscreant characters corrupted; how many times has the company they keep affected children. The Prophet ﷺ said: 'A person is in the religion of his close companion. So each one should look to whom he takes as a close friend.'

Don't ask about a person, but ask about his close friends,

because every friend follows his companion.

Fifth: Nurture the child to seek success and maturity. Create in his heart a love for sublime aspirations. Ignite hatred for all that is indecent. The Prophet Muhammad ﷺ said: 'Verily Allah loves the most noble of affairs and He despises the most trivial of them.' Do not incline the child or leave him to imitate women and the decadent. For this will become his greatest regret and disgrace.

Sixth: Observe the child in his dress and appearance. That he should observe the mores of the Muhammadan way completely and not imitate the enemies of Allah. The Prophet ﷺ pointed out: 'Whoever imitates a people, he is from among them.' Accordingly, Muslim men should avoid the wearing of gold and silk, or dragging their garments on the ground. They should shun instability and despair in their conversations as well as excessive laughter, merriment, fickleness, haste, feeble-mindedness, time-wasting and other such faults and defects.

Seventh: Exalt the affairs of Allah and all that relates to His religion in the heart of the child. The parent should also sanctify Allah's names, qualities and actions. He should recognize Him as free of all defects and display this to his child, instilling in him the greatness of Allah, His Quran, and noble Messenger ﷺ.

Eighth: Encourage the child to seek useful knowledge. The parent should help him to be serious and sincere in this undertaking. And, likewise, to sacrifice, preserve and repeat it. Make the child feel that the fruits of ripe knowledge and its alluring results are good enough reason to rise upon from slumber and negligence.

Ninth: To pray for him to be successful in every prayer and desire from Allah, that He should reform and guide him by the hand. To implore in the early hours of the morning and at the times when prayers are granted that Allah should write faith in his heart and help him with his angels. Allah Almighty says: 'And those who pray: "O Our Sustainer! Grant that our spouses and our offspring be a joy to our eyes, and cause us to be foremost among those who are conscious of Thee!"' (25:74).

وَٱلَّذِينَ يَقُولُونَ رَبَّنَا هَبْ لَنَا مِنْ أَزْوَٰجِنَا وَذُرِّيَّٰتِنَا قُرَّةَ أَعْيُنٍ وَٱجْعَلْنَا لِلْمُتَّقِينَ إِمَامًا

Tenth: Show kindness and mercy to children. Bestow upon them gentle emotions by playing with them, kissing them and entering into their hearts' happiness. Do not be harsh and dispassionate with them. Neither should you hurt or embarrass them in front of people. Every Muslim should treat his children the way the Prophet Muhammad ﷺ did. For those who show mercy Allah will show mercy upon them.

O Allah! Bless us wherever we are. Grant that our spouses and our offspring be a joy to our eyes, and cause us to be foremost among those who are conscious of Thee.

Lesson 19

The occurrence of waste during Ramadan

Waste is one of the sins and wrong-doing that the deviant nations have fallen into. Allah Almighty has forbidden and condemned it. 'And do not waste [God's bounties]: verily, He does not love the wasteful!' (6:141).

وَهُوَ ٱلَّذِىٓ أَنشَأَ جَنَّٰتٍ مَّعۡرُوشَٰتٍ وَغَيۡرَ مَعۡرُوشَٰتٍ وَٱلنَّخۡلَ وَٱلزَّرۡعَ مُخۡتَلِفًا أُكُلُهُۥ وَٱلزَّيۡتُونَ وَٱلرُّمَّانَ مُتَشَٰبِهٗا وَغَيۡرَ مُتَشَٰبِهٖۚ كُلُواْ مِن ثَمَرِهِۦٓ إِذَآ أَثۡمَرَ وَءَاتُواْ حَقَّهُۥ يَوۡمَ حَصَادِهِۦۖ وَلَا تُسۡرِفُوٓاْۚ إِنَّهُۥ لَا يُحِبُّ ٱلۡمُسۡرِفِينَ

Waste is a custom of people who do not revere Allah. They do not respect His bounties. In spite of His warning: 'But do not squander [thy substance] senselessly. Behold, the squanderers are, indeed, of the ilk of the satans – in as much as Satan has indeed proved most ungrateful to his Sustainer' (17:26–7).

وَءَاتِ ذَا ٱلۡقُرۡبَىٰ حَقَّهُۥ وَٱلۡمِسۡكِينَ وَٱبۡنَ ٱلسَّبِيلِ وَلَا تُبَذِّرۡ تَبۡذِيرًا ۝ إِنَّ ٱلۡمُبَذِّرِينَ كَانُوٓاْ إِخۡوَٰنَ ٱلشَّيَٰطِينِۖ وَكَانَ ٱلشَّيۡطَٰنُ لِرَبِّهِۦ كَفُورٗا

Many people waste a great deal in Ramadan.

Among the various forms of squander is the preparation of excessive food above natural needs. Some people are accustomed to many kinds of food and drink. In Ramadan they load their dining tables in the early morning and evening with everything that is delicious and good. Most of it is left to spoil and is thereafter thrown away.

O you who fast! Be aware of extravagance and waste! There are poor and needy people among the Muslims. Give, therefore, whatever you have in excess to the indigent servants of Allah, perhaps this would be registered for you with Allah Almighty. He says of His servants: 'Who gives food – however great be their own want of it – unto the needy, and the orphan, and the captive, [saying, in their hearts] "We feed you for the sake of God alone: we desire no recompense from you, nor thanks: Behold, we stand in awe of our Sustainer's judgement on a distressful, fateful day!"' (76:8–10).

وَيُطْعِمُونَ ٱلطَّعَامَ عَلَىٰ حُبِّهِۦ مِسْكِينًا وَيَتِيمًا وَأَسِيرًا ۝ إِنَّمَا نُطْعِمُكُمْ لِوَجْهِ ٱللَّهِ لَا نُرِيدُ مِنكُمْ جَزَآءً وَلَا شُكُورًا ۝ إِنَّا نَخَافُ مِن رَّبِّنَا يَوْمًا عَبُوسًا قَمْطَرِيرًا

The Prophet Muhammad says in an authentic *hadith* that: on the Day of Judgement Allah Almighty will say: 'O son of man! I was hungry and you fed me not.' The servant will reply: 'How could I have fed You and You are Lord of all the worlds?' Allah will say: 'Did you not know that my servant, so and so, was hungry and did not feed him? If you fed him, you would have found that with Me.'

Among the various forms of extravagance is that of excessive sleep way above normal needs, especially in the day. Many people who fast turn their days into spells of deep slumber and negligence. And, strange as it may seem, they spend many hours staying up at night pursuing matters all too much to account for. They waste their nights in gossip and trivialities. Others spend their nights engaged in things that are totally unlawful and abominable, thereby provoking the anger of Allah Almighty.

Another kind of extravagance that is often witnessed is the time and money spent in preparing for *Eid al Fitr* – the Festival of the Breaking of the Fast. Many Muslims incur expenses far above their ability to pay. They squander huge sums of money on clothes, games and other forms of preparations. Indeed, it is quite common to find people who spend thousands upon thousands upon these vanities when, in reality, they are the meanest of persons when it comes to giving charity and other acts of righteousness.

O you whom Allah has blessed with wealth! Know that in society there are orphans and poor people. Will you not feed the hungry and clothe the naked? Will you not build a mosque? Will you not contact someone with whom your relationship was broken? Will you not relieve the distress from one who is afflicted?

Still another form of waste is the indulgence by those who fast in numerous visits without any gain or benefit. Similarly, they engage in mixing repeatedly with people for no specific reason or interest. In this way, their time is wasted, their age is frittered away and their days are lost. The Quran forewarns that on the Day of Judgement such people will cry: 'Alas for us, that we disregarded it!' (8:31).

وَإِذَا تُتْلَىٰ عَلَيْهِمْ ءَايَٰتُنَا قَالُوا۟ قَدْ سَمِعْنَا لَوْ نَشَآءُ لَقُلْنَا مِثْلَ هَٰذَآ إِنْ هَٰذَآ إِلَّآ أَسَٰطِيرُ ٱلْأَوَّلِينَ

Further waste is witnessed in the addiction to entertainment and recreation. Hence the obsession with games such as football, physical exercises, picnics and other activities that consume valuable time that could have otherwise been devoted to worship, remembrance of Allah, recitation of the Quran, acquisition of knowledge, propagation, and enjoining good and forbidding wrong. In this light, it is evident that many people squander their time in the strangest ways; yet, tomorrow when the graves throw up what they contain and the hearts reveal what they bear, all these people will see the results of their actions.

On the whole, the various forms of extravagance can be summarized as follows:

- People who waste their time in disobedience and sin. Their extravagance is the most dangerous and worst kind.

- People who waste their time by aimlessly strewing it in all directions. They will be most regretful on the Day of the Great Exhibition.

- People who waste time and money on food, drink and clothes which do not increase them except in dejection and anxiety.

- People who waste their time in the permissible games, amusement and picnics. They have, in reality, cheated their age.

We ask Allah for success, steadfastness, guidance and strict economy.

Lesson 20

Ramadan: the month of righteousness and contact

Fasting brings about a softening of the heart and a humbling of self. It increases the individual in mercy and compassion. The people most deserving of the mercy and goodness of those who fast are his relatives and family members. Ramadan reminds the Muslim of his relatives, in-laws and offspring. Thus he visits them, contacts them, and shows love to them. Allah says: '[Ask them:] "Would you, perchance, after having turned away [from God's commandment, prefer to revert to your old ways, and] spread corruption on earth, and [once again] cut asunder your ties of kinship?" (47:22).

$$\text{فَهَلْ عَسَيْتُمْ إِن تَوَلَّيْتُمْ أَن تُفْسِدُوا فِى ٱلْأَرْضِ وَتُقَطِّعُوٓا۟ أَرْحَامَكُمْ}$$

To cut asunder ties of kinship is, therefore, a major sin. It is one of the most detestable mistakes and calamities. Maintaining contact with one's relatives is one of the best deeds and greatest demonstrations of righteousness. One wise man of old said:

Surely, that which is between me and my father's
relatives and between myself and my uncle's
relatives is quite different.

If they violate my honour, I will protect their
honour.

If they destroy my reputation, I will build
their reputation.

And I will never bear any old grudge for them,
For the patron of a people never bears ill will.

Also in this regard the noble Prophet ﷺ said: 'No one who cuts asunder the ties of kinship will enter Paradise.' And how will such a person enter Paradise after they have cut what Allah ordered them to maintain. Again the Prophet ﷺ said: 'When Allah created the womb it hung unto the throne and said: "This is the station of the one who seeks refuge in You from being cut off." Allah said: "Do you not wish that I shall reach out to whomsoever reaches out to you and cut off whomsoever severs ties with you?" The womb said: "Yes." Then Allah said: "That shall be granted to you."'

Prophet Muhammad also said: 'The one who maintains relations is not he who reciprocates but it is he who contacts those who sever ties with him.' Likewise a man once said to the Prophet ﷺ: 'O Messenger of Allah, I have relatives whom I contact but they sever ties with me. I do well to them but they treat me unkindly.' The Prophet said: 'If the matter is the way you narrate it, then it is like if you fed them with hot ashes and you still have support from Allah.'

With the exception of a few, the majority of the Prophet's ﷺ relatives were among his most implacable enemies. They expelled him from his home, pursued him, denied him of his rights, punished him and waged war against him. Yet, when Allah granted him victory over them, he granted them a pardon that was unparalleled at the time.

Maintaining contact with relatives increases one's age, elevates it, purifies it and multiplies its rewards abundantly. It is, moreover, a sign of complete faith, awe of Al Rahman – the Most Gracious – and implementation of the Quran. In the same manner, preserving kindred ties acts as a shield for the individual in the battles against evil and disgrace in this world and in the Hereafter. It was narrated in one tradition: 'Verily Allah ordered me to contact whomsoever severs ties with me and give to whomsoever denies me.'

The greatest relationship and most exalted closeness is that of righteousness, generosity and devotion to parents. It involves prayers for them and obedience in matters that do not lead to disobedience of Allah. 'For thy Sustainer has ordained that you shall worship none but Him. And do good unto [thy] parents. Should one of them or both, attain to old age in thy care, never say "Ugh" to them or scold, but [always] speak unto them with reverent speech, and spread over them humbly the wings of thy tenderness, and say: "O my Sustainer! Bestow Thy grace upon them, even as they cherished and reared me when I was a child!" (17:24).

وَٱخْفِضْ لَهُمَا جَنَاحَ ٱلذُّلِّ مِنَ ٱلرَّحْمَةِ وَقُل رَّبِّ ٱرْحَمْهُمَا كَمَا رَبَّيَانِى صَغِيرًا

A man once came to the Prophet ﷺ and asked: 'O Messenger of Allah, who is most deserving of my companionship?' The Prophet said: 'Your mother.' The man said: 'Then who?' The Prophet said: 'Your mother.' The man again asked: 'Then who?' And the Prophet repeated: 'Your mother.' Finally the man asked: 'Then who?' And the Prophet replied: 'Your father.'

An ungrateful son once did wrong to his father, insulted him and denied the good that he had done for him. The father wept and moaned saying:

> I looked after your health as a babe and held hopes
> for you in adolescence, as you busied yourself with
> all that befell you.
>
> If the night tormented you with illness I never slept,
> but remained restless and suffering
> because of your illness.
>
> As if I were the afflicted and not you,
> though it was you and not me my eyes
> cried profusely.
>
> And when you became of age and fulfilled
> the ambition for which you strove and I hoped
>
> You made my reward hostility and harshness,
> as if you are the Bestower of all good and favour.

Fasting is perhaps the greatest school for learning righteousness and preserving contact with relatives. It is a spring from which good character flows, a tributary of mercy and a rope of kindness. Fasting amends and purifies the souls of those who fast. Their feelings and entire beings are improved and mobilized. Let us, therefore, return to our relatives in this month and embrace them with visits, overwhelm them with affection, prayers and togetherness. And surely Allah will not cause us to lose the reward of those who do good.

O Allah! Grant us understanding of our religion and plant us firm in the traditions of the leader the God-fearing and guide us to the one and only correct path.

Lesson 21

Ramadan: the month of mercy

Mercy is a favour from Allah which He places in the hearts of whomsoever He wills. Verily, Allah will have mercy on His servants who are merciful. Allah is the Most Compassionate the Most Merciful. He loves the merciful and calls to mercy. He orders His servants to enjoin patience and mercy. A person may lack mercy for any number of reasons, among them, an abundance of sins and disobedience. They stain their hearts so much so that they ultimately blind them until their hearts become harder than stones. Allah says of the Children of Israel: 'And yet, after all this, your hearts hardened and became like rocks, or even harder' (2:74).

ثُمَّ قَسَتْ قُلُوبُكُم مِّنۢ بَعْدِ ذَٰلِكَ فَهِيَ كَٱلْحِجَارَةِ أَوْ أَشَدُّ قَسْوَةً ۚ وَإِنَّ مِنَ ٱلْحِجَارَةِ لَمَا يَتَفَجَّرُ مِنْهُ ٱلْأَنْهَٰرُ ۚ وَإِنَّ مِنْهَا لَمَا يَشَّقَّقُ فَيَخْرُجُ مِنْهُ ٱلْمَآءُ ۚ وَإِنَّ مِنْهَا لَمَا يَهْبِطُ مِنْ خَشْيَةِ ٱللَّهِ ۗ وَمَا ٱللَّهُ بِغَٰفِلٍ عَمَّا تَعْمَلُونَ

Allah also says about them when they opposed and rebelled against the divine law: 'Then, for having broken their solemn pledge, We rejected them and caused their hearts to harden' (5:13).

$$\text{فَبِمَا نَقْضِهِم مِّيثَٰقَهُمْ لَعَنَّٰهُمْ وَجَعَلْنَا قُلُوبَهُمْ قَٰسِيَةً ۖ يُحَرِّفُونَ ٱلْكَلِمَ عَن مَّوَاضِعِهِۦ ۙ وَنَسُوا۟ حَظًّا مِّمَّا ذُكِّرُوا۟ بِهِۦ ۚ وَلَا تَزَالُ تَطَّلِعُ عَلَىٰ خَآئِنَةٍ مِّنْهُمْ إِلَّا قَلِيلًا مِّنْهُمْ ۖ فَٱعْفُ عَنْهُمْ وَٱصْفَحْ ۚ إِنَّ ٱللَّهَ يُحِبُّ ٱلْمُحْسِنِينَ}$$

Among the things that cause a loss of mercy is arrogance with wealth and pride with riches. Allah says: 'Nay, verily, man becomes grossly overweening whenever he believes himself to be self-sufficient' (96:6–7).

$$\text{كَلَّآ إِنَّ ٱلْإِنسَٰنَ لَيَطْغَىٰٓ أَن رَّءَاهُ ٱسْتَغْنَىٰٓ}$$

The day the heart is disciplined with faith and good deeds it fills with mercy and kindness.

Another reason for the weakness of mercy is an abundance of gluttony and saturation. They give rise to contempt and recklessness. Hence the month of fasting was prescribed to crush this unruliness and ill discipline. The fasting person is naturally among the most merciful people. That is because he has tasted hunger, experienced thirst and endured hardship. His soul is, therefore, enveloped with mercy, care and gentleness for Muslims.

Mercy is something which every Muslim is required to render to his brother Muslim. It is a requirement from every responsible custodian toward those under his care. He should feel sorry for them and be lenient toward them. Prophet Muhammad ﷺ said: 'O Allah! Whoever was entrusted with authority over any affair of the Muslims and made it difficult for them, please make it difficult for him. And whoever was entrusted over any affair of the Muslims and was kind toward them, then be kind toward him.'

In a related *hadith* Allah's Messenger also said: 'Whoever oversees an affair for my nation and disappeared or abandoned them without fulfilling their needs while impoverishing them, Allah will debar him from his needs and impoverish him on the Day of Judgement.'

Mercy demands that the scholar and teacher should be gentle toward his students and lead them to the easiest and best ways to love him and benefit from his teachings. If he does this Allah will decree for him the most excellent and abounding reward. Listen to the manner in which Allah praises His Prophet ﷺ: 'And it was by God's grace that thou [O Prophet] didst deal gently with thy followers: for if thou hadst been harsh and hard of heart, they would indeed have broken away from thee' (3:159).

$$\text{فَبِمَا رَحْمَةٍ مِنَ اللَّهِ لِنْتَ لَهُمْ وَلَوْ كُنْتَ فَظًّا غَلِيظَ الْقَلْبِ لَانْفَضُّوا مِنْ حَوْلِكَ فَاعْفُ عَنْهُمْ وَاسْتَغْفِرْ لَهُمْ وَشَاوِرْهُمْ فِي الْأَمْرِ فَإِذَا عَزَمْتَ فَتَوَكَّلْ عَلَى اللَّهِ إِنَّ اللَّهَ يُحِبُّ الْمُتَوَكِّلِينَ}$$

Mercy further requires from the imam that he should not make worship difficult for his followers or cause them harm. On the contrary, he should be merciful, kind and wise. The Prophet ﷺ said: 'Whoever from you leads the people in prayer must make it easy because among them are the old, the sick, the young and the needy.' It was narrated that when Mu'adh once extended the prayer the Prophet ﷺ said to him: 'Are you a troublemaker O Mu'adh? Are you a troublemaker O Mu'adh? Are you a troublemaker O Mu'adh?'

In the same manner, when Uthman ibn Abi al As al Thaqafi requested: 'O Messenger of Allah, make me an imam of my people.' The Prophet ﷺ said: 'You are their imam so lead the prayer according to the weakest of them and take a caller to prayer who would seek no payment for doing so.'

Mercy dictates that the one who calls to Islam must advise

those whom he is inviting with tenderness. That he should, moreover, clarify issues to them with concern. He should not hurt, defame people or even revile the disobedient in public. Allah advised Moses and Aaron to employ the following methods in their call to the tyrant Pharaoh: 'But speak unto him in a mild manner, so that he might bethink himself or [at least] be filled with apprehension' (20:44).

$$\text{فَقُولَا لَهُ قَوْلًا لَّيِّنًا لَّعَلَّهُ يَتَذَكَّرُ أَوْ يَخْشَىٰ}$$

He also says: 'Call thou [all mankind] unto thy Sustainer's path with wisdom and goodly exhortation, and argue with them in the most kindly manner' (16:125).

$$\text{ادْعُ إِلَىٰ سَبِيلِ رَبِّكَ بِالْحِكْمَةِ وَالْمَوْعِظَةِ الْحَسَنَةِ وَجَادِلْهُم بِالَّتِي هِيَ أَحْسَنُ إِنَّ رَبَّكَ هُوَ أَعْلَمُ بِمَن ضَلَّ عَن سَبِيلِهِ وَهُوَ أَعْلَمُ بِالْمُهْتَدِينَ}$$

The eminent jurist and Islamic scholar, Imam al Shafe'e wrote:

> Support me with your advice in private,
> and avoid advising me in public.
>
> Surely giving advice among the people is a kind of reproach,
> which I would rather not listen to.
>
> If you disobey and ignore my wish,
> don't be saddened if you are not obeyed.

Mercy is required from a father to his children. This matter was previously discussed in the lesson (No. 18) on how we train our children. The mercy of the father or mother toward her children has the greatest effect on their integrity, well-being and obedience. Self-praise and harshness only open the door to despair. The Prophet ﷺ said: 'Kindness was never bestowed upon something except that it beautified it, and it was never removed from that thing except that it made it ugly.'

O you who fast and cause hunger to your stomach, there are thousands of stomachs more awaiting a meal. Will there not arise from among you those who would feed them? O you who fast and cause thirst to your liver, there are thousands more who await a mouthful of water. Will there not arise from among you those who would quench their thirst? O you who fast and wear the finest garments, there are naked people out there awaiting only a piece of cloth to cover their bodies. Will there not then come forth from among you those who would clothe them?

O Allah! We implore your extended mercy that will forgive our sins and erase our misdeeds and errors.

Lesson 22

How can we revive the traditions in Ramadan?

The leader and model of the Islamic nation is Prophet Muhammad ﷺ. There is no happiness except through following him. No prosperity can be achieved except by following in his footsteps. Allah Almighty says: 'Those who shall follow the [last] Apostle, the unlettered Prophet whom they shall find described in the Torah that is with them, and [later on] in the Gospel: [the Prophet] who will enjoin upon them the doing of what is right and forbid them the doing of what is wrong, and make lawful to them the good things of life and forbid them the bad things' (7:157).

ٱلَّذِينَ يَتَّبِعُونَ ٱلرَّسُولَ ٱلنَّبِيَّ ٱلْأُمِّيَّ ٱلَّذِى يَجِدُونَهُۥ مَكْتُوبًا عِندَهُمْ فِى ٱلتَّوْرَىٰةِ وَٱلْإِنجِيلِ يَأْمُرُهُم بِٱلْمَعْرُوفِ وَيَنْهَىٰهُمْ عَنِ ٱلْمُنكَرِ وَيُحِلُّ لَهُمُ ٱلطَّيِّبَٰتِ وَيُحَرِّمُ عَلَيْهِمُ ٱلْخَبَٰٓئِثَ وَيَضَعُ عَنْهُمْ إِصْرَهُمْ وَٱلْأَغْلَٰلَ ٱلَّتِى كَانَتْ عَلَيْهِمْ ۚ فَٱلَّذِينَ ءَامَنُوا۟ بِهِۦ وَعَزَّرُوهُ وَنَصَرُوهُ وَٱتَّبَعُوا۟ ٱلنُّورَ ٱلَّذِىٓ أُنزِلَ مَعَهُۥٓ ۙ أُو۟لَٰٓئِكَ هُمُ ٱلْمُفْلِحُونَ

After his coming, no one will enter Paradise except by following his way. His Sunnah (way) is like the ship of Noah. Whoever boards it will be saved. Whomsoever turns his back on it will be destroyed. Allah says: 'Verily, in the Apostle of God you have a good example for everyone who looks forward [with hope and awe] to God and the Last Day, and remembers God unceasingly' (33:21).

لَقَدْ كَانَ لَكُمْ فِى رَسُولِ ٱللَّهِ أُسْوَةٌ حَسَنَةٌ لِّمَن كَانَ يَرْجُواْ ٱللَّهَ وَٱلْيَوْمَ ٱلْءَاخِرَ وَذَكَرَ ٱللَّهَ كَثِيرًا

In a moving sermon that brought tears to the eyes of his companions, the Prophet ﷺ said: 'You must keep to my Sunnah and the Sunnah of the Rightly Guided Caliphs – cling to them stubbornly. Beware of newly invented matters, for every invented matter is an innovation and every innovation is a going astray.' He also said: 'Whomsoever desires other than my way is not from me.' And: 'He who does an act with which our matter is not [in agreement] will have it rejected.'

Still on the importance of following His Messenger, Allah Almighty says: 'Now whenever God and His Apostle have decided a matter, it is not for a believing man or a believing woman to claim freedom of choice insofar as they themselves are concerned' (33:36).

وَمَا كَانَ لِمُؤْمِنٍ وَلَا مُؤْمِنَةٍ إِذَا قَضَى ٱللَّهُ وَرَسُولُهُۥ أَمْرًا أَن يَكُونَ لَهُمُ ٱلْخِيَرَةُ مِنْ أَمْرِهِمْ وَمَن يَعْصِ ٱللَّهَ وَرَسُولَهُۥ فَقَدْ ضَلَّ ضَلَٰلًا مُّبِينًا

In another chapter of the Noble Quran Allah prohibited the presentation of oneself before Himself and the Prophet: 'O you who have attained to faith! Do not put yourselves forward in the presence of [what] God and His Apostle [may have ordained]' (49:1).

يَٰٓأَيُّهَا ٱلَّذِينَ ءَامَنُواْ لَا تُقَدِّمُواْ بَيْنَ يَدَىِ ٱللَّهِ وَرَسُولِهِۦ وَٱتَّقُواْ ٱللَّهَ إِنَّ ٱللَّهَ سَمِيعٌ عَلِيمٌ

The month of Ramadan is a blessed season in which to revive the pure traditions within the self, home and society.

Concerning the general traditions which the fasting Muslim must effect and uphold at all times, they include what was authenticated by Imam Muslim and the other five imams in their collections (Sahih Bukhari, Sunan ibn Majah, Sunan Abu Daud, Jam'e al Tirmidhi, and Sunan al Nisa'e) that the Prophet ﷺ said: 'Ten things are from natural disposition. Cutting the moustache, allowing the beard to grow, inhaling water, cutting the finger and toe nails, washing the knuckles, clipping the hairs of the armpit, shaving the pubic hairs, and being prudent in the use of water.'

It was also confirmed that the Prophet ﷺ prohibited the dragging of one's lower garments on the ground. According to this directive in the collection of Imam Muslim, Allah's Messenger said: 'Allah will not look at the one who drags his garment on the ground out of vanity.' In a related *hadith* he further warned: 'What is below the ankle is in the fire.'

The authentic books of *hadith* also establish that the Prophet ﷺ prohibited many things. According to a *hadith* narrated by Anas in the collections of Muslim, Abu Daud, and Al Tirmidhi, he forbade: 'That a man should stand and drink.' Likewise, in another *hadith* narrated by Ibn Umar and collected by Bukhari, the Prophet ﷺ forbade: 'That a man should stand and then sit in his seat' (to greet or show respect to someone else). Also, in a *hadith* narrated by Jabir in the collection of Al Nisa'e he prohibited: 'The male from touching his penis with his right hand, from walking in the shoe of a female, wearing a garment turned upside down, sitting with one's legs drawn up and wrapped in one's garment without anything covering one's private parts.' Furthermore, Ahmad transmitted on the authority of Abu

Sa'eed that the Prophet ﷺ: 'Forbade that a man should walk in the shoe or slippers of a female.' Sahal ibn Sa'eed narrated that Allah's Messenger: 'Prohibited blowing into a drink' (Al Tabarani). Anas again narrated (Al Nisa'e) that Prophet Muhammad ﷺ: 'Forbade eating and drinking from gold and silver wares.' Both Imams Ahmad and Al Nisa'e transmitted an authentic *hadith* in which the Prophet: 'Forbade men from wearing gold and silk; but allowed them for women.'

On matters relating to worship, the Prophet ﷺ forbade the performance of prayer between *al Fajr* – the morning prayer and the rising of the sun; and between *al Asr* the mid-afternoon prayer and the setting of the sun (Bukhari and Muslim). Anas narrated that he also forbade the offering of prayers to graves (Ibn Hibban – *sahih*) He prohibited sleep before *al Esha* – the night prayer.

He forbade:

- loud wailing (Abu Daud – *hadith sahih*)

- plucking off the gray hair (Al Tirmidhi, Al Nisa'e, Ibn Majah – *sahih*)

- fasting on Friday – (Yaum ul Jumu'ah) by itself (Bukhari and Muslim)

- the selling of surplus water (Muslim).

- tattooing (Ahmad – *sahih*)

Among the established traditions is that the Prophet used a small stick (*siwak*) to clean and polish his teeth. He said: 'If I did not want to make it difficult for my nation I would have ordered them to clean their teeth [do *siwak*] during every ablution.' In other *hadiths* it says at the performance of every prayer. The Prophet ﷺ also said: 'Cleaning the teeth with *siwak* purifies the mouth and earns the pleasure of the Lord.'

Other notable traditions include the offering of two units (*raka'atyn*) in prayer of salutation to the mosque before sitting in it. One should enter the mosque with the right foot and leave with the left. He should wear his right shoe first and take of the left side first. A visitor must seek permission to enter by knocking or greeting three times. If permission is not granted the visitor should go away. This was confirmed in a *sahih hadith*. Altogether these *ahadith* point to practical and daily traditions.

O Allah! Help us to follow the way of the Prophet ﷺ, effect, and preserve them.

Lesson 23

Letter to Muslim woman on the occasion of Ramadan.

Allah Almighty has praised believing Muslim women who are patient and humble. He describes them as women who guard the intimacy which He ordained to be guarded. When He mentions the qualities of the righteous men He says: 'And thus does their Sustainer answer their prayer: I shall not lose sight of the labour of any of you who labours [in My way], be it man or woman; each of you is an issue of the other' (3:195).

فَٱسْتَجَابَ لَهُمْ رَبُّهُمْ أَنِّى لَآ أُضِيعُ عَمَلَ عَـٰمِلٍ مِّنكُم مِّن ذَكَرٍ أَوْ أُنثَىٰ ۖ بَعْضُكُم مِّنۢ بَعْضٍ ۖ فَٱلَّذِينَ هَاجَرُوا۟ وَأُخْرِجُوا۟ مِن دِيَـٰرِهِمْ وَأُوذُوا۟ فِى سَبِيلِى وَقَـٰتَلُوا۟ وَقُتِلُوا۟ لَأُكَفِّرَنَّ عَنْهُمْ سَيِّـَٔاتِهِمْ وَلَأُدْخِلَنَّهُمْ جَنَّـٰتٍ تَجْرِى مِن تَحْتِهَا ٱلْأَنْهَـٰرُ ثَوَابًا مِّنْ عِندِ ٱللَّهِ ۗ وَٱللَّهُ عِندَهُۥ حُسْنُ ٱلثَّوَابِ

On this occasion of Ramadan I bring glad tidings to you young women of Islam. Salutations to you nation of Allah with the onset of this month. May Allah make it a month of forgiveness and sincere repentance for all of us. Please accept from us on this occasion, dear sister, a bouquet of advice that has sprouted from ten roses:

First: he Muslim woman believes in Allah as her Lord, Muhammad ﷺ as Prophet, and Islam as her religion and way of life. She manifests the impact of faith upon her in speech, deeds and beliefs. She is ever cautious not to provoke the anger of Allah, fears His painful punishment and the consequences of going against His commands.

Second: the Muslim woman performs her five daily prayers with ablutions and with humility at the prescribed times. No preoccupation or amusement distracts her from prayers. The effects of prayer are thus clearly manifested in her personality. For prayers prevent the conduct of indecency and wrong-doing; it is the great fortress standing in the way of disobedience.

Third: the Muslim woman maintains her covering and is honoured to commit herself to it. She does not go out except being fully covered and yet seeking the cover of Allah. She thanks Him for favouring her with this cover that has both protected and purified her. Allah says: 'O Prophet! Tell thy wives and thy daughters, as well as all [other] believing women, that they should draw over themselves some of their outer garments [when in public]' (33:59).

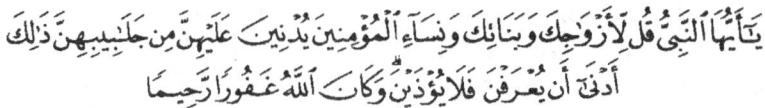

Fourth: the Muslim woman is vigilant in obedience of her husband. She is tender and merciful toward him; invites him to goodness, advises him and ensures that he is always comfortable. She does not raise her voice to him and neither does she ever display harshness in her speech toward her husband. The Prophet ﷺ said: 'If a woman prays her five prayers, fasts in the month of Ramadan and obeys her husband, she will enter the Paradise of her Lord.'

Fifth: the Muslim woman raises her children in obedience to Allah. She nurtures them with the milk of correct doctrine. She implants in their hearts the love of Allah Most High and His Prophet ﷺ. Additionally, the Muslim mother helps her children to avoid the ways of disobedience and indecent behaviour. Allah Almighty says: 'O you who have attained to faith! Ward off from yourselves and those who are close to you that fire [of the hereafter] whose fuel is human beings and stones: [lording] over it are angelic powers awesome [and] severe, who do not disobey God in whatever He has commanded them, but [always] do what they are bidden to do' (66:6).

يَٰٓأَيُّهَا ٱلَّذِينَ ءَامَنُوا۟ قُوٓا۟ أَنفُسَكُمْ وَأَهْلِيكُمْ نَارًا وَقُودُهَا ٱلنَّاسُ وَٱلْحِجَارَةُ عَلَيْهَا مَلَٰٓئِكَةٌ غِلَاظٌ شِدَادٌ لَّا يَعْصُونَ ٱللَّهَ مَآ أَمَرَهُمْ وَيَفْعَلُونَ مَا يُؤْمَرُونَ

Sixth: the Muslim woman does not allow herself to be alone in any situation with a strange man. The Prophet ﷺ said: 'A woman does not find herself alone with a (marriageable) man except that Satan is the third party of their company.' Accordingly, the Muslim woman does not travel without the company of an unmarriageable person. She does not roam the markets and public places without necessity. And when she does so, she remains fully covered and modest.

Seventh: the Muslim woman does not imitate a man in things that are specific and peculiar to him. Prophet Muhammad ﷺ said: 'Allah has cursed the men who imitate women and the women who imitate men.' She does not imitate the unbelieving women in their dress, fashions and appearances. As the Prophet ﷺ said: 'Whoever imitates a people he is from among them.'

Eighth: the Muslim woman calls to Allah within the ranks of her women-folk with good words, visits her neighbours and contacts her sisters through telephone calls or with Islamic booklets and cassettes. She practises what she preaches and tries earnestly to save herself and her sisters form the punishment of Allah. The Prophet ﷺ observed: 'That Allah should guide to Islam one person through your effort is better than a caravan of wealth.'

Ninth: the Muslim woman protects her heart from doubtful matters and desires, as well as her eyes from unlawful things. Likewise, she protects her ears from music and indecency and all her limbs from wrong-doing. She knows that this is piety. As the Prophet ﷺ advised: 'Be modest and have a sense of shame before Allah as best as you can. Whoever is truly modest before Allah will safeguard his head with all that it knows and the stomach with what it contains. And, whomsoever remembers the trials of life would leave the delights of this world.'

Tenth: the Muslim woman does not waste her time; neither does she cause her days and nights to be shredded apart. She does not allow herself to become a backbiter, slanderer or castigator indulging in negligence. Allah says: 'And leave to themselves all those who, beguiled by the life of this world, have made play and passing delights their religion' (6:70).

وَذَرِ ٱلَّذِينَ ٱتَّخَذُوا۟ دِينَهُمْ لَعِبًا وَلَهْوًا وَغَرَّتْهُمُ ٱلْحَيَوٰةُ ٱلدُّنْيَا وَذَكِّرْ بِهِۦٓ أَن تُبْسَلَ نَفْسٌۢ بِمَا كَسَبَتْ لَيْسَ لَهَا مِن دُونِ ٱللَّهِ وَلِىٌّ وَلَا شَفِيعٌ وَإِن تَعْدِلْ كُلَّ عَدْلٍ

$$\text{لَا يُؤْخَذُ مِنْهَا ۚ أُو۟لَٰٓئِكَ ٱلَّذِينَ أُبْسِلُوا۟ بِمَا كَسَبُوا۟ ۖ لَهُمْ شَرَابٌ مِّنْ حَمِيمٍ وَعَذَابٌ أَلِيمٌ بِمَا كَانُوا۟ يَكْفُرُونَ}$$

He also says, concerning the people who wasted their lives, that they will ultimately say: 'Alas for us, that we disregarded it' (6:31).

$$\text{قَدْ خَسِرَ ٱلَّذِينَ كَذَّبُوا۟ بِلِقَآءِ ٱللَّهِ ۖ حَتَّىٰٓ إِذَا جَآءَتْهُمُ ٱلسَّاعَةُ بَغْتَةً قَالُوا۟ يَٰحَسْرَتَنَا عَلَىٰ مَا فَرَّطْنَا فِيهَا وَهُمْ يَحْمِلُونَ أَوْزَارَهُمْ عَلَىٰ ظُهُورِهِمْ ۚ أَلَا سَآءَ مَا يَزِرُونَ}$$

O Allah! Guide the young women of Islam to that which You love and are pleased with and beautify their hearts with faith.

Lesson 24

Concerns of the Islamic scholar during the month of Ramadan

Allah Almighty declares in the Quran: 'Verily, [O you who believe in Me,] this community of yours is one single community, since I am the Sustainer of you all: worship, then, Me [alone]' (21:92).

$$\text{إِنَّ هَٰذِهِۦ أُمَّتُكُمْ أُمَّةً وَٰحِدَةً وَأَنَا۠ رَبُّكُمْ فَٱعْبُدُونِ}$$

He further explains: 'All believers are but brethren' (49:10).

$$\text{إِنَّمَا ٱلْمُؤْمِنُونَ إِخْوَةٌ فَأَصْلِحُوا۟ بَيْنَ أَخَوَيْكُمْ وَٱتَّقُوا۟ ٱللَّهَ لَعَلَّكُمْ تُرْحَمُونَ}$$

As for the Prophet ﷺ, he clarified the nature of the relationship between Muslims in this famous *hadith*: 'The example of the Muslims in their love and mercy for each other is like the body. If one part is afflicted, all the other parts rally to its aid with fever and sleeplessness.'

Today Muslims pass this month of Ramadan in

transgression and crises.

Capitalism is rife with greed. It directs its hostility against the Islamic world with intellectual onslaughts. The foremost means toward this is through women, wine and other enticements, distractions, luxuries and unlawful amusements.

Secularism calls for the separation between the religion and worldly affairs. It seeks to oust Islam from life's stage on the pretext that religion distinguishes between people. In effect, secularism is an atheist ideology that disregards all religions and, therefore, excludes Islam in its entirety from playing any role in human life.

Freemasonry, the Jewish creation, has come to destroy religions including Islam. On the surface it appears to be calling for the unity of all people. It has its own means, taboos, emblems and cliques. It operates in secret, has world-wide influence and springs from Zionist origins.

Hence today the Islamic nation suffers from intense wounds:

- Palestine has been stolen from it, Al Aqsa mosque remains a hostage while old men, women and children are slaughtered morning and evening. Yet, Palestine will never be returned to the Muslim lands except by an Islam with the rage of Umar ibn al Khattab, the boldness of Salah al Din and the sincerity of Ibn Taymiya.

- The Muslim woman is fought against because of her covering, modesty, purity and religion.

- Our young men are seduced by destructive means, satanic enticements and sensual delights.

- Evangelism is penetrating the Islamic world from all

four directions.

- Divisions and schisms are widespread among Muslims except those whom Allah has shielded.

In the circumstances, what is required is that the Muslim should live for these great issues with his sentiments, wealth and prayers. He should strive to increase awareness among his Muslim brothers of these dangers. The Muslim should work relentlessly to bring about unity within the ranks of his own community. More importantly, the Islamic nation must avoid disputes and internal wrangling that only cause failure; particularly when the news of these calamities which afflict the Islamic world are exposed and become the issues of the day. As a result, no Muslim should despise himself because in every Muslim there is good.

Indeed, every Muslim is expected to struggle if he or she is able and to stop making excuses. They must strive with their persons and their wealth. If not, with their wealth and the support of others who spend of their wealth to advance the cause of Islam. They should, at the end of each prayer, in the early hours of the morning, and other times when prayers are answered, implore Allah to establish and grant victory to the Muslims. We must, moreover, all call upon Allah to increase us in piety and God-consciousness because the disasters and calamities that have befallen us are all on account of our sins and shortcomings. 'And do you, now that a calamity has befallen you after you had inflicted twice as much [on your foes], ask yourselves, "How has this come about?" Say: "It has come from your own selves"' (3:165).

أَوَلَمَّآ أَصَٰبَتۡكُم مُّصِيبَةٞ قَدۡ أَصَبۡتُم مِّثۡلَيۡهَا قُلۡتُمۡ أَنَّىٰ هَٰذَاۖ قُلۡ هُوَ مِنۡ عِندِ أَنفُسِكُمۡۗ إِنَّ ٱللَّهَ عَلَىٰ كُلِّ شَيۡءٖ قَدِيرٞ

In the past the Islamic nation was accustomed to victories and conquests in Ramadan. But, after, it reneged on its mission and became engrossed in worldly delights. Ramadan became in recent years a time of anxiety, sadness, killing, dispersal and genocide. Of course if we return to Allah we shall be victorious. 'O you who have attained to faith! If you help [the cause of] God, He will help you, and will make firm your steps' (47:7).

يَٰٓأَيُّهَا ٱلَّذِينَ ءَامَنُوٓا۟ إِن تَنصُرُوا۟ ٱللَّهَ يَنصُرْكُمْ وَيُثَبِّتْ أَقْدَامَكُمْ

'No succour can come from any save God, the Almighty, the Truly Wise' (3:126).

وَمَا جَعَلَهُ ٱللَّهُ إِلَّا بُشْرَىٰ لَكُمْ وَلِتَطْمَئِنَّ قُلُوبُكُم بِهِۦ ۗ وَمَا ٱلنَّصْرُ إِلَّا مِنْ عِندِ ٱللَّهِ ٱلْعَزِيزِ ٱلْحَكِيمِ

'If God succours you, none can ever overcome you' (3:160).

إِن يَنصُرْكُمُ ٱللَّهُ فَلَا غَالِبَ لَكُمْ ۖ وَإِن يَخْذُلْكُمْ فَمَن ذَا ٱلَّذِى يَنصُرُكُم مِّنۢ بَعْدِهِۦ ۗ وَعَلَى ٱللَّهِ فَلْيَتَوَكَّلِ ٱلْمُؤْمِنُونَ

Allah! We implore of You the help that You have promised us. O Our Lord! Plant our feet firmly and grant us victory over the unbelieving people.

Lesson 25

Ramadan calls for the preservation of time

Allah describes the discourse between Himself and the reckless and negligent on the Day of Judgement: '[And] He will ask [the doomed]: "What number of years have you spent on earth?" They will answer: "We have spent there a day, or part of a day; but ask those who [are able to] count time... .[Whereupon] He will say: "You have spent there but a short while: had you but known [how short it was to be]! Did you then think that We created you in mere idle play, and that you not have to return to Us? [Know,] then, [that] God is sublimely exalted, the Ultimate Sovereign, the Ultimate Truth: there is no deity save Him, the Sustainer, in bountiful almightiness enthroned!"' (23:112–16).

قَـٰلَ كَمْ لَبِثْتُمْ فِى ٱلْأَرْضِ عَدَدَ سِنِينَ ۝ قَالُوا۟ لَبِثْنَا يَوْمًا أَوْ بَعْضَ يَوْمٍ فَسْـَٔلِ ٱلْعَآدِّينَ ۝ قَـٰلَ إِن لَّبِثْتُمْ إِلَّا قَلِيلًا ۖ لَّوْ أَنَّكُمْ كُنتُمْ تَعْلَمُونَ ۝ أَفَحَسِبْتُمْ أَنَّمَا خَلَقْنَـٰكُمْ عَبَثًا وَأَنَّكُمْ إِلَيْنَا لَا تُرْجَعُونَ ۝ فَتَعَـٰلَى ٱللَّهُ ٱلْمَلِكُ ٱلْحَقُّ ۖ لَآ إِلَـٰهَ إِلَّا هُوَ رَبُّ ٱلْعَرْشِ ٱلْكَرِيمِ

One of the righteous predecessors noted: life is short, do not shorten it with negligence. This is, certainly, true. Negligence shortens the hours and consumes the night. Hence the Prophet ﷺ said: 'Two favours that many people are deceived by: health and spare time.' The lesson being that many people are healthy and have a lot of time on their hands yet their lives pass by quickly before them without their using them or benefiting anyone. He also warned: 'The foot of a believer will not move on the Day of Judgement until he is asked about four things and mention his life span and how he utilized it.' Life is, undoubtedly, a treasure, whomsoever spends it in obedience to Allah will find his treasure on the Day when wealth and sons will be of no avail but instead only those who returned to Allah with clean hearts. Thus, those who spent their lives in negligence, disobedience and play will on that Day regret in such a manner that will never be equalled thereafter. They will say: 'Alas for us, that we disregarded our lives.'

In effect, both the night and day are like riding animals that transport man to either eternal happiness or loss. Our righteous forbears used to take every initiative to preserve their time. There are strange stories about them concerning this matter. There were among them those who used to read the Quran and they were on the threshold of death. Such an example was Junaid ibn Muhammad. His sons said to him, 'You are exhausting yourself.' He replied, 'And should there be among the people one who exerts himself more than me?'

Al Aswad ibn Yazid used to stand in prayer for most of the night. Some of his friends advised him to relax at least for a small portion of the night. He told them it is this very relaxation he is in search of; meaning in the Hereafter.

Sufiyan al Thowri once sat in the Sacred Mosque speaking to some people. Then suddenly he arose terrified and said; we are sitting here and the day is doing its work. There were among our forbears those who used to divide their days and nights into hours. Hence they allocated specific hours for prayers, recitation, remembrance, meditation, acquisition of knowledge, work and sleep. They ascribed no time for merriment.

As for their successors, they have been afflicted by the calamity of time-wasting. Except, of course, those to whom Allah has shown mercy. They indulge in excessive sleep, idleness, aimless wandering, spending on amusements and sittings in which there is no benefit; or in meetings which, if they do not involve disobedience, are definitely the cause of disobedience.

Among the greatest things that organize time and work are the five daily prayers. Allah the Sublime and Most Excellent Speaker affirms in the Quran: 'Verily, for all believers prayer is indeed a sacred duty linked to particular times [of day]' (4:104).

وَلَا تَهِنُوا۟ فِى ٱبْتِغَآءِ ٱلْقَوْمِ ۖ إِن تَكُونُوا۟ تَأْلَمُونَ فَإِنَّهُمْ يَأْلَمُونَ كَمَا تَأْلَمُونَ ۖ وَتَرْجُونَ مِنَ ٱللَّهِ مَا لَا يَرْجُونَ ۗ وَكَانَ ٱللَّهُ عَلِيمًا حَكِيمًا

The month of Ramadan is a school in which the Muslim's time is organized and invested in matters that lead to closeness to Allah. Notwithstanding, some people do not know the meaning of fasting. They engage in ample negligence and deep slumber. They spend their days sleeping and their nights in wasted wakefulness.

O Allah! Preserve for us our lives. Plant our feet firmly on Your path, and make us obey You always. O Lord of all the worlds.

Lesson 26

Images of love and brotherhood are manifested in Ramadan

The Muslims constitute one hand, one heart and one unit. They are like the Prophet ﷺ described them, as a single body. Only Islam can gather their disparate elements. And, only Islam can create brotherhood between them. 'If thou hadst expended all that is on earth, thou couldst not have brought their hearts together [by thyself]: but God did bring them together. Verily, He is Almighty, wise' (8:63).

وَأَلَّفَ بَيْنَ قُلُوبِهِمْ لَوْ أَنفَقْتَ مَا فِي ٱلْأَرْضِ جَمِيعًا مَّا أَلَّفْتَ بَيْنَ قُلُوبِهِمْ وَلَٰكِنَّ ٱللَّهَ أَلَّفَ بَيْنَهُمْ إِنَّهُ عَزِيزٌ حَكِيمٌ

Significantly, the Muslims are not united in language, blood, colour, race or country; they possess, however, unity of religion. For they are all brought together under the umbrella of 'There is no God save Allah and Muhammad is the Messenger of Allah.'

Muslims distinguish themselves by their God-consciousness and gain precedence because of their knowledge. 'O men! Behold, We have created you all out of a male and a female, and have made you into nations and tribes, so that you might come to know one another. Verily, the noblest of you in the sight of God is the one who is most deeply conscious of Him. Behold, God is all-knowing, all-aware' (49:13).

يَٰٓأَيُّهَا ٱلنَّاسُ إِنَّا خَلَقْنَٰكُم مِّن ذَكَرٍ وَأُنثَىٰ وَجَعَلْنَٰكُمْ شُعُوبًا وَقَبَآئِلَ لِتَعَارَفُوٓا۟ إِنَّ أَكْرَمَكُمْ عِندَ ٱللَّهِ أَتْقَىٰكُمْ إِنَّ ٱللَّهَ عَلِيمٌ خَبِيرٌ

When the Prophet ﷺ called to Islam, the caller to prayer came from Ethiopia saying, 'Here I am O Lord, I have answered your call.' Likewise, the Prophet himself came forth and proclaimed concerning Salman the Persian: 'Salman is from my household.' And, there was Shuaib the Roman, calling, 'God is the greatest, God is the greatest.' Meanwhile, the people of segregation and racism, Al Walid ibn Mughira, Abu Jahl and Abu Lahab all regressed.

Thus it was reported that the Prophet ﷺ used to say: 'O children of Hashim, a people would come on the Day of Judgement with their deeds and you would come with your family trees.' In another *hadith* he warned: 'Whoever was slowed down by his deeds would not be hastened by his lineage.'

In reality, the Muslims constitute a large brotherhood in which every righteous and guided believer gains membership. Islam does not belong to one particular people or race. It belongs to the Arabs, Indians, Turks, Pakistanis and Africans; indeed all mankind. Abu Bakr al Siddiq was a Qurayshi, Bilal an Ethiopian, Shuaib a Roman, Salman a Persian and Muhammad the Conqueror was a Turk. Iqbal the great poet was an Indian and Salah al Din al Ayubi was a Kurd. They were all bonded by the same doctrine;

that there is no God save Allah and Muhammad is the Messenger of Allah.

This great oneness manifests itself in Ramadan. The month is one and the same, the fasting is one, the direction of prayers is one, and the methodology is also one. We all pray behind one imam. Allah says: 'And bow down in prayer with all who thus bow down' (2:43).

$$\text{أَتَأْمُرُونَ ٱلنَّاسَ بِٱلْبِرِّ وَتَنسَوْنَ أَنفُسَكُمْ وَأَنتُمْ تَتْلُونَ ٱلْكِتَٰبَ أَفَلَا تَعْقِلُونَ}$$

And: 'Stand before God in devout obedience' (2:238).

$$\text{حَٰفِظُوا۟ عَلَى ٱلصَّلَوَٰتِ وَٱلصَّلَوٰةِ ٱلْوُسْطَىٰ وَقُومُوا۟ لِلَّهِ قَٰنِتِينَ}$$

Addressing those who fast, Allah Almighty says: 'O you who have attained to faith! Fasting is ordained for you as it was ordained for those before you, so that you might remain conscious of God' (2:183).

$$\text{يَٰٓأَيُّهَا ٱلَّذِينَ ءَامَنُوا۟ كُتِبَ عَلَيْكُمُ ٱلصِّيَامُ كَمَا كُتِبَ عَلَى ٱلَّذِينَ مِن قَبْلِكُمْ لَعَلَّكُمْ تَتَّقُونَ}$$

In the same manner, our pilgrimage is one, its timing is one, and its venue is one. 'And when you surge downward in multitudes from Arafat, remember God at the holy place, and remember Him as the One who guided you after you had indeed been lost on your way' (2:198).

$$\text{لَيْسَ عَلَيْكُمْ جُنَاحٌ أَن تَبْتَغُوا۟ فَضْلًا مِّن رَّبِّكُمْ فَإِذَآ أَفَضْتُم مِّنْ عَرَفَٰتٍ فَٱذْكُرُوا۟ ٱللَّهَ عِندَ ٱلْمَشْعَرِ ٱلْحَرَامِ وَٱذْكُرُوهُ كَمَا هَدَىٰكُمْ وَإِن كُنتُم مِّن قَبْلِهِۦ لَمِنَ ٱلضَّآلِّينَ}$$

Allah further calls upon the Muslims to maintain His bond

and not to be divided: 'And hold fast, all together, unto the bond with God, and do not draw apart from one another. And remember the blessings which God has bestowed upon you: how, when you were enemies, He brought your hearts together, so that through His blessing you became brethren' (3:103).

وَٱعْتَصِمُوا۟ بِحَبْلِ ٱللَّهِ جَمِيعًا وَلَا تَفَرَّقُوا۟ وَٱذْكُرُوا۟ نِعْمَتَ ٱللَّهِ عَلَيْكُمْ إِذْ كُنتُمْ أَعْدَآءً فَأَلَّفَ بَيْنَ قُلُوبِكُمْ فَأَصْبَحْتُم بِنِعْمَتِهِۦٓ إِخْوَٰنًا وَكُنتُمْ عَلَىٰ شَفَا حُفْرَةٍ مِّنَ ٱلنَّارِ فَأَنقَذَكُم مِّنْهَا كَذَٰلِكَ يُبَيِّنُ ٱللَّهُ لَكُمْ ءَايَٰتِهِۦ لَعَلَّكُمْ تَهْتَدُونَ

In forbidding divisions, Allah says: 'And be not like those who have drawn apart from one another and have taken to conflicting views after all evidence of the truth has come unto them: for these it is for whom tremendous suffering is in store' (3:105).

وَلَا تَكُونُوا۟ كَٱلَّذِينَ تَفَرَّقُوا۟ وَٱخْتَلَفُوا۟ مِنۢ بَعْدِ مَا جَآءَهُمُ ٱلْبَيِّنَٰتُ وَأُو۟لَٰٓئِكَ لَهُمْ عَذَابٌ عَظِيمٌ

One practical measure that must be adopted as a means of preventing divisions is contained in the Prophet's saying: 'Allah has revealed to me that you should be humble so that no one will oppress another and no one will display arrogance toward another.' In another *hadith* Allah's Messenger said: 'The believers are like bricks in a wall; they support each other.' He also said: 'A Muslim is the brother of a Muslim: he neither oppresses him nor does he fail him, he neither lies to him nor does he hold him in contempt. It is evil enough for a man to hold his brother Muslim in contempt. The whole of a Muslim for another is inviolable: his blood, his property, and his honour.'

Among the duties of this brotherhood is that one should

inquire about the well-being of his brother and visit him for the sake of Allah. He should, moreover, visit and console him if he is sick, greet him whenever he meets him with a bright smile on his face, pray for him when he sneezes, accept his invitation, help him if he is oppressed, and advise and direct him. There are, of course, other rights and duties. Every Muslim on the face of the earth is, therefore, your brother in faith and according to the Quranic law. Allah Almighty has originated this covenant which Prophet Muhammad ﷺ brought.

O Allah! Attune our hearts, bring us together, and unite our ranks. O You who are the most generous to those who show kindness.

Lesson 27

Ramadan is a blessed month for the Islamic call

The propagation of Islam was the mission of all the prophets and messengers of Allah. There was never a prophet who was not a preacher and teacher. All of them preached the same message: 'Worship Allah, you have no other god but Him.' They all called to their people saying: 'I do not seek any reward from you for this work.'

Allah Almighty says: 'Call thou [all mankind] unto thy Sustainer's path with wisdom and goodly exhortation, and argue with them in the most kindly manner' (16:125).

ادْعُ إِلَىٰ سَبِيلِ رَبِّكَ بِٱلْحِكْمَةِ وَٱلْمَوْعِظَةِ ٱلْحَسَنَةِ وَجَٰدِلْهُم بِٱلَّتِى هِىَ أَحْسَنُ إِنَّ رَبَّكَ هُوَ أَعْلَمُ بِمَن ضَلَّ عَن سَبِيلِهِۦ وَهُوَ أَعْلَمُ بِٱلْمُهْتَدِينَ

He ordered His Messenger: 'Say [O Prophet]: "This is my way: resting upon conscious insight accessible to reason, I am calling [you all] unto God – I and they who follow me." And [say] "Limitless is God in His glory; and I am not one of those who ascribe divinity to aught beside Him!"' (12:108).

$$\text{قُلْ هَٰذِهِۦ سَبِيلِىٓ أَدْعُوٓا۟ إِلَى ٱللَّهِ عَلَىٰ بَصِيرَةٍ أَنَا۠ وَمَنِ ٱتَّبَعَنِى وَسُبْحَٰنَ ٱللَّهِ وَمَآ أَنَا۠ مِنَ ٱلْمُشْرِكِينَ}$$

Having ordered his servants to employ useful knowledge and good deeds, Allah confirms: 'And who could be better of speech than he who calls [his fellow-men] unto God, and does what is just and right, and says, "Verily, I am of those who have surrendered themselves to God?' (41:33).

$$\text{وَمَنْ أَحْسَنُ قَوْلًا مِّمَّن دَعَآ إِلَى ٱللَّهِ وَعَمِلَ صَٰلِحًا وَقَالَ إِنَّنِى مِنَ ٱلْمُسْلِمِينَ}$$

There are five premises to the Islamic call, it has five approaches, and its results are also five.

The five premises:

First: sincerity and truthfulness with Allah, and to seek His favour. Allah says: 'And withal, they were not enjoined aught but that they should worship God, sincere in their faith to Him alone' (98:5).

$$\text{وَمَآ أُمِرُوٓا۟ إِلَّا لِيَعْبُدُوا۟ ٱللَّهَ مُخْلِصِينَ لَهُ ٱلدِّينَ حُنَفَآءَ وَيُقِيمُوا۟ ٱلصَّلَوٰةَ وَيُؤْتُوا۟ ٱلزَّكَوٰةَ وَذَٰلِكَ دِينُ ٱلْقَيِّمَةِ}$$

The holy Prophet ﷺ foretold that the first with whom the fire of hell will be lit are three; among them a scholar who acquired knowledge so that people would say he is learned. And it was indeed said of him.

Second: to practise what one preaches. Actually it is a scandal and disgrace that a person's actions should contradict his words. Allah derides such people in His Quran: 'Do you bid other people to be pious, the while you forget your own selves – and yet you recite the divine writ? Will you not, then, use your reason?' (2:44).

وَٱسْتَعِينُوا۟ بِٱلصَّبْرِ وَٱلصَّلَوٰةِ وَإِنَّهَا لَكَبِيرَةٌ إِلَّا عَلَى ٱلْخَٰشِعِينَ

Third: gentleness in presenting the message. Allah advised Moses and Aaron to adopt this measure with Pharaoh, the greatest tyrant of his time: 'But speak unto him in a mild manner, so that he might bethink himself or [at least] be filled with apprehension' (20:44).

فَقُولَا لَهُۥ قَوْلًا لَّيِّنًا لَّعَلَّهُۥ يَتَذَكَّرُ أَوْ يَخْشَىٰ

And to Muhammad, He also cautioned: 'And it was by God's grace that thou [O Prophet] didst deal gently with thy followers: for if thou hadst been harsh and hard of heart, they would indeed have broken away from thee' (3:159).

فَبِمَا رَحْمَةٍ مِّنَ ٱللَّهِ لِنتَ لَهُمْ وَلَوْ كُنتَ فَظًّا غَلِيظَ ٱلْقَلْبِ لَٱنفَضُّوا۟ مِنْ حَوْلِكَ فَٱعْفُ عَنْهُمْ وَٱسْتَغْفِرْ لَهُمْ وَشَاوِرْهُمْ فِى ٱلْأَمْرِ فَإِذَا عَزَمْتَ فَتَوَكَّلْ عَلَى ٱللَّهِ إِنَّ ٱللَّهَ يُحِبُّ ٱلْمُتَوَكِّلِينَ

Hence it was on this basis the Prophet ﷺ declared: 'Make matters easy and do not make them difficult. Give glad tidings and do not drive people away.'

Fourth: adopt a gradual approach to propagation. Do as Prophet Muhammad ﷺ did in his mission by beginning with the most important matters; then follow them up in order of priority. This was clearly demonstrated in the advice he gave to Mu'adh before he sent him to Yemen. 'You will come upon a People of the Book (Jews and Christians), the first thing you should invite them to is to bear witness that there is no God save Allah and that I am the Messenger of Allah. If they respond positively to this, then inform them that Allah had ordained for them five prayers each day and night.'

Fifth: address every people with what is suited for them and their needs. There is a special approach to the people of the cities and another approach to villagers. Similarly, there is a special approach to the bedouin. The intellectual has his position and the ignorant also has his position. So too, there is a style for the argumentative and an entirely different one for the submissive. 'And whoever is granted wisdom has indeed been granted wealth abundant' (2:269).

$$\text{يُؤْتِي الْحِكْمَةَ مَن يَشَاءُ وَمَن يُؤْتَ الْحِكْمَةَ فَقَدْ أُوتِيَ خَيْرًا كَثِيرًا وَمَا يَذَّكَّرُ إِلَّا أُوْلُوا الْأَلْبَابِ}$$

The five means of propagation:

First: the individual method; that is, to invite the person individually if the matter pertains to him specifically.

Second: public or mass propagation such as in lectures or exhortations that benefit the generality of people.

Third: private lessons to students each in his speciality. This is the task of the scholars who specialize in their disciplines.

Fourth: propagation through writing, correspondence and authorship with guidance and benefit for those who are called.

Fifth: propagation using modern means of communication to advance the cause of truth.

The five results:

First: to attain the position of inheritors of the prophets, for they were the first callers and beacons of light in the field of propagation.

Second: to obtain prayers for your forgiveness from the creation for having taught the people goodness. Even the whale in the ocean will pray for the caller to truth.

Third: to gain great rewards equivalent to that of those who are invited. The Prophet ﷺ said: 'Whoever calls to a good tradition will have the reward as the one who followed it without reducing from their reward.'

Fourth: the development of the caller from being one who is called to one who calls. He influences others and is not influenced by others who call to evil.

Fifth: the caller will become a leader among his people and they will follow him. Allah Almighty describes the righteous and notes that they call upon Him saying: 'Cause us to be foremost among those who are conscious of Thee!' (25:74).

وَٱلَّذِينَ يَقُولُونَ رَبَّنَا هَبْ لَنَا مِنْ أَزْوَٰجِنَا وَذُرِّيَّٰتِنَا قُرَّةَ أَعْيُنٍ وَٱجْعَلْنَا لِلْمُتَّقِينَ إِمَامًا

Surely the sentiments of the caller to Islam are awakened in Ramadan. Their tongues are put to use and their pens become unstinting. The podiums welcome them to hear their call and addresses. Are there not any other scholars who will be similarly generous with their knowledge so that Allah will cause benefit from it?

    O Allah! Increase us in useful Knowledge, righteous deeds and understanding of religion.

Lesson 28

The prayer of the fasting person is never refused

Prophet Muhammad ﷺ conveyed this in a well-known saying: 'To the fasting person there is a prayer that is never refused.' That is because the heart of the fasting person is repentant. He has subdued his stubbornness and checked his wild ambitions. Indeed, he has drawn closer to his Lord and obeyed Him. He abandoned his food and drink, fearful of the King, the Bestower. The fasting person has restrained his desires in obedience to the Lord of the heavens and the earth. The Prophet ﷺ said: 'Supplication is worship.' Thus, if you see a servant begging a lot in prayer, know that he is close to Allah and confident in His Lord.

The companions once said to the Prophet: 'O Messenger of Allah, is our Lord near so that we may confide with Him secretly or is He far that we must cry out to Him?' Thereupon Allah Almighty revealed the following verse of the Quran: 'And if My servants ask thee about Me – behold, I am near; I respond to the call of him who calls, whenever he calls unto Me: let them, then, respond unto Me, and believe in Me, so that they might follow the right way' (2:186).

وَإِذَا سَأَلَكَ عِبَادِى عَنِّى فَإِنِّى قَرِيبٌ أُجِيبُ دَعْوَةَ ٱلدَّاعِ إِذَا دَعَانِ فَلْيَسْتَجِيبُوا۟ لِى وَلْيُؤْمِنُوا۟ بِى لَعَلَّهُمْ يَرْشُدُونَ

In this same regard the Prophet ﷺ said to his companions: 'You are not calling upon a deaf or absent God. Verily you are calling upon a hearer and seer who is closer to any of you than the neck of his camel.' Supplication is an extended rope and solid divine bond. Hence the Prophet ﷺ declared: 'No one will be destroyed with supplication.' For this reason Allah Most Merciful exhorts us to call upon Him: 'Call upon your Sustainer humbly, and in the secrecy of your hearts. Verily, He loves not those who transgress the bounds of what is right' (7:55).

ٱدْعُوا۟ رَبَّكُمْ تَضَرُّعًا وَخُفْيَةً إِنَّهُ لَا يُحِبُّ ٱلْمُعْتَدِينَ

And: 'Call unto Me, [and] I shall respond to you! Verily, they who are too proud to worship Me will enter hell, abased!' (40:60).

وَقَالَ رَبُّكُمُ ٱدْعُونِى أَسْتَجِبْ لَكُمْ إِنَّ ٱلَّذِينَ يَسْتَكْبِرُونَ عَنْ عِبَادَتِى سَيَدْخُلُونَ جَهَنَّمَ دَاخِرِينَ

Still, the Prophet ﷺ said: 'Our Lord descends to the heavens of the earth in the last third of the night and says: "Is there one who asks that I may grant him his request, is there one who would call that I may answer him, and is there one who seeks forgiveness that I may forgive him?"'

Ramadan is the month of supplication, attainment, repentance and acceptance. O faster whose his lips have dried from fasting, whose liver craved from thirst, and whose stomach hungered; call upon your Lord in earnest and be insistent in your request. Remember Allah's description of His righteous servants: 'They would vie with one another in doing good works, and would call unto Us in yearning and awe; and they were always humble before Us' (21:90).

فَٱسْتَجَبْنَا لَهُۥ وَوَهَبْنَا لَهُۥ يَحْيَىٰ وَأَصْلَحْنَا لَهُۥ زَوْجَهُۥٓ إِنَّهُمْ كَانُوا۟ يُسَٰرِعُونَ فِى ٱلْخَيْرَٰتِ وَيَدْعُونَنَا رَغَبًا وَرَهَبًا وَكَانُوا۟ لَنَا خَٰشِعِينَ

There are certain ethics of supplication that the fasting person should know. They include: the resolve of the heart and full trust in the generosity and favour of Allah. The Prophet ﷺ said: 'None of you should say, "O my Lord forgive me if You will." He should instead be insistent in his asking because nothing forces Allah.' Among these ethics also is that the servant should praise Allah and send greetings upon his noble Messenger ﷺ at the beginning, in the middle and at the end of his supplication. The believer should be conscious of the times when prayers are answered such as the last third of the night, while prostrating, between the call to prayer (*Azaan*) and its commencement (*Iqamah*), at the end of the compulsory prayers, the last hour of Friday (*Yaum-ul-Jum'uah*), after the *Asr* prayer, and on the day of *Arafat*. The believer must avoid rhymed prose in supplication, assigning someone to do it, or excesses in it. One should be careful not to invoke sin or the cutting of kindred ties.

O You who fast, know that the final hour before the setting of the sun is one of the greatest hours of the day.

Before the breaking of the fast when hunger has become acute and your thirst most intense, make much supplication, increase your yearning and continue to ask. Note that there is also an hour before daybreak for you who fast. Therefore, be good to yourself and ask from the Ever-Living the Self-Subsisting because you are poor and He is rich, you are weak and He is strong, you will pass away and He will remain.

The Prophet Abraham prayed: 'O my Sustainer, cause me and [some] of my offspring to remain constant in prayer! And, O our Sustainer, accept this my prayer: grant Thy forgiveness unto me, and my parents, and all the believers, on the Day on which the [last] reckoning will come to pass!' (14: 40–1).

رَبِّ ٱجْعَلْنِى مُقِيمَ ٱلصَّلَوٰةِ وَمِن ذُرِّيَّتِى رَبَّنَا وَتَقَبَّلْ دُعَآءِ ۝ رَبَّنَا ٱغْفِرْ لِى وَلِوَٰلِدَىَّ وَلِلْمُؤْمِنِينَ يَوْمَ يَقُومُ ٱلْحِسَابُ

Prophet Moses prayed: 'O my Sustainer! Open up my heart [to Thy light], and make my task easy for me' (20:25).

قَالَ رَبِّ ٱشْرَحْ لِى صَدْرِى

Prophet Solomon called upon his Lord and asked: 'O my Sustainer! Forgive my sins, and bestow upon me the gift of a kingdom which may not suit anyone after me: verily, Thou alone art a giver of gifts!' (38:35).

قَالَ رَبِّ ٱغْفِرْ لِى وَهَبْ لِى مُلْكًا لَّا يَنۢبَغِى لِأَحَدٍ مِّنۢ بَعْدِىٓ إِنَّكَ أَنتَ ٱلْوَهَّابُ

In an authentic *hadith* the Prophet Muhammad prayed: 'O my Sustainer! You are the Lord of Gabriel, Mika'il, and Israfil. You are the maker of the heavens and the earth. You judge between Your servants in what they differ. Guide me to the truth by Your permission. For You guide whomsoever You will to the straight path.'

There are four advantages of supplication:

First: the realization of worship of Allah Almighty, humbleness towards Him and trust in Him. This is the purpose and fruit of worship.

Second: the answering of one's request either through the granting of good or by the prevention of harm. None other than Allah possesses this power and ability.

Third: to save the reward with Allah if the request is not granted in this world. This is actually better and more beneficial.

Fourth: supplication expresses sincere monotheism through the crushing of dependency on people and yearning for their favour.

O our Lord! Grant us good in this world and good in the Hereafter and save us from the punishment of the fire. O our Lord! Do not cause our hearts to go astray after You have guided us and grant us mercy from Yourself. Verily You are the Donor of all Good.

Lesson 29

Gifts to those who fast

At this stage I can not find a better gift or greater masterpiece than to present to those who fast gifts from the Prophet of guidance ﷺ. They are those practical *hadith*s that have been mentioned in connection with rewards and blessings. Behold! They are the *hadith*s that lead to the doors of happiness and the paths of goodness in this world and the Hereafter.

O you who fast! Record these *hadith*s and implement them: The Prophet ﷺ said: 'Whoever says at daybreak: "There is no God save Allah alone, He has no partner, to Him belongs the dominion and the praise and He has power over all things"; such a person will have the equivalent of a slave from the son of Ismail; ten good deeds will be written for him, ten misdeeds will be erased, and he will be elevated ten levels. He will be protected from Satan until evening, and if he says it in the evening, he would have the same rewards until morning' (Ahmad, Abu Daud, Ibn Majah – *sahih*).

The Prophet # also said: 'Whoever says in the morning

or in the evening: "O Allah! You are my Lord. There is no God beside You. You created me and I am Your slave and I have taken a covenant to You and promised You what I am able to do. I seek refuge with You from the evil of what I have done, I acknowledge Your favour upon me and I acknowledge my sin. Forgive me because none forgives sins except You." If a servant died during the day or night after having said this prayer, he will enter Paradise' (Ahmad, Abu Daud, Al Nisa'e, Ibn Majah, Ibn Hibban, Al Hakim – *sahih*; Al Bukhari transmits another version of this *hadith*).

Again the Prophet ﷺ said: 'Whoever says at morning or evening: "Glory and praise be Allah the Great" one hundred times, no one will come forward on the Day of Judgement with better than he; except if someone said the same as him and added to it' (Muslim, Ahmad, Abu Daud, Al Tirmidhi).

'Whoever said: "Glory and praise be to Allah the Great", a date tree will be planted for him in the Paradise' (Al Tirmidhi, Ibn Hibban, Al Hakim – *sahih*).

'Whoever says: "Glory and praise be to Allah" one hundred times in a single day his sins would be erased even if they were like the waves of the sea' (Bukhari and Muslim).

'Whoever implements ten verses of the Quran will not be included among the negligent. Whoever implements one hundred verses will be considered among the obedient. And, whoever implements one thousand verses will be among he extremely rich' (Abu Daud, Ibn Hibban – *sahih*).

'Whoever says in the evening: "In the name of Allah with whose name there can be no harm in the earth or in the heavens and He is the Hearer the Knower" three times, he will not be afflicted with a sudden calamity before morning. And whoever says it in the morning three times will not be afflicted with a sudden calamity before evening' (Abu Daud, Ibn Hibban, Al Hakim – *sahih*).

'Whoever says: "I seek refuge with the perfect words of Allah from the evil that He created" three times in the evening will not be harmed by the bite of a serpent during that night' (Al Tirmidhi, Ibn Hibban, Al Hakim – *sahih*).

'Whoever says upon leaving his house: "In the name of Allah, I trust in Allah, there is no movement and no power except with Allah", it would be said to him: "You have been contented and you took precaution", Satan will turn away from him' (Al Tirmidhi, Abu Daud, Ibn Hibban, Ibn al Sunni – *sahih*).

'Whoever says when he hears the caller to prayer: "And I bear witness that there is no God save Allah, He is alone and has no partner and I bear witness that Muhammad is His servant and messenger. I am pleased with Allah as Lord, Muhammad as Prophet and Islam as religion" all his sins will be forgiven' (Muslim and the other five).

'Whoever recites the Surah al Ikhlas ten times, Allah will build for him a house in the Paradise' (Ahmad – *sahih*).

'Whoever recites the Surah al Khaf on a Friday, a light will be created for him until the next Friday' (Al Hakim and Al Bayhaqi – *sahih*).

'Whoever recites the verse of the throne after every compulsory prayer will not be forbidden entrance to Paradise' (Ibn Hibban and Al Nisa'e – *sahih*).

'Whoever recites Surah al Ikhlas it is as if he read one-third of the Quran' (Ahmad, Al Nisa'e, Al Tirmidhi – *sahih*).

This bouquet from Muhammad ﷺ we grant to all those who fast.

O Allah! Help us to remember You, thank You and worship You in the best way. Amen.

Lesson 30

Tomorrow is Eid - the festival of the breaking of the fast

Tomorrow is Eid and Eid is tomorrow. What is the meaning of Eid and how will it be? Eid is not for him who wears new clothes. Or who takes pride in his affluence. Surely Eid is for those who feared the Promised Day of Reckoning and the owner of the Majestic Throne.

Eid is not rhythms and strings. It is not arbitrary amusement and wildness. Eid is rather an occasion of gratitude to the Beneficent and acknowledgement of His favour. It is a time to display His grace and advance in the convoy of believers, strengthening the religion and overcoming the enemies of Islam.

The affairs of Eid include:

One should eat something before the Eid prayer. This may take the form of dates in accord with the command of Allah as was demonstrated while fasting. Likewise, the alms for the breaking of the fast (*Zakaat al Fitr*) acquits the fasting person from mistakes and obscenities committed during Ramadan. It brings happiness to the poor, revives the spirit of cooperation and kindness among Muslims, purifies their souls and suppresses their tendencies toward stinginess.

Wearing new clothes and perfumes is one of the practices of Eid. It is a means of recognizing the kindness of Allah Almighty. It involves beautification because Allah is beautiful and he loves that which is beautiful. Eid is a time to display the favour of Allah as there is a *hadith* that says: 'Verily Allah loves to see the effect of His favour upon His servant if He blesses him.' It is an occasion to exchange visits, greetings, love and good wishes. It demands contact with relatives, kindness to parents, empathy for the poor and compassion for neighbours.

The Muslim Eid reflects happiness that is governed by the Islamic rules and mores. It enjoins dignified fun, courteous and innocent games, caring smiles, legitimate picnics and creative stories. This is an occasion that evokes images of the Day of the Great Exhibition. Eid gathers thousands upon thousands of rich, poor, big, small, ruler, ruled, happy and sad.

Eid is a day of rewards. Whoever fasted with faith and consciousness grant him glad tidings of a great prize, a major success and a huge reward. Whosoever sinned while fasting, was careless with the command of Allah and transgressed His boundaries, he will regret it and feel deeply sorry. And what a great loss that would be.

On the day of Eid there will be two groups of people returning from the prayer. One group has been rewarded and is grateful. Allah will say to them: 'Go you have been forgiven. You pleased Me and I have been pleased with you.'

The other group is that of the losers and despondent. They will be returning with disappointment, loss, regret, and denial.

One righteous man passed by a group of people engaged in vain conversation and having fun on Eid day. He said to them: 'If you did well in Ramadan, this is not gratitude for goodness. And, if you wronged, this is not the way of one who has erred with the most Merciful.'

Umar ibn Abdul Aziz saw some people hastening away from Arafat on their horses and camels at sunset. He said to them, 'The one who wins not he who goes fastest on his horse or camel; but the winner is he whose sins are forgiven.' O Muslim! Think about those with whom you prayed last Eid. They included your fathers, grandfathers, beloved ones and friends. Where are they? Where have they gone? Tomorrow you will receive the prize. Tomorrow you will be given your full recompense in a record of your deeds. Make sure that only good is written in it. And, await your greatest Eid. The day when you would win the pleasure and forgiveness of Allah by His permission. 'He that shall be drawn away from the fire and brought into Paradise will indeed have gained a triumph: for the life of this world is nothing but an enjoyment of self-delusion' (3:185).

كُلُّ نَفْسٍ ذَآئِقَةُ ٱلْمَوْتِ وَإِنَّمَا تُوَفَّوْنَ أُجُورَكُمْ يَوْمَ ٱلْقِيَٰمَةِ فَمَن زُحْزِحَ عَنِ ٱلنَّارِ وَأُدْخِلَ ٱلْجَنَّةَ فَقَدْ فَازَ وَمَا ٱلْحَيَوٰةُ ٱلدُّنْيَآ إِلَّا مَتَٰعُ ٱلْغُرُورِ

Conclusion

O you who fast! May the peace, blessings and mercy of Allah be upon you. I entrust you in God's care, the One who does not cause to lose anything in His trust. May your fasting and standing in prayer at nights be good. Enjoy what you have striven for.

Allah Almighty says: '[But,] behold, as for those for whom [the decree of] ultimate good has already gone forth from Us – these will be kept far away from that [hell]: no sound thereof will they hear; and they will abide in all that their souls have ever desired' (21:101–2).

إِنَّ ٱلَّذِينَ سَبَقَتْ لَهُم مِّنَّا ٱلْحُسْنَىٰٓ أُو۟لَـٰٓئِكَ عَنْهَا مُبْعَدُونَ ۝ لَا يَسْمَعُونَ حَسِيسَهَا ۖ وَهُمْ فِى مَا ٱشْتَهَتْ أَنفُسُهُمْ خَـٰلِدُونَ

May Allah make you and I among them, and accept from us all our deeds. Surely Allah knows best. And may His peace and blessings be upon Muhammad, his relatives and companions.

www.ingramcontent.com/pod-product-compliance
Lightning Source LLC
Chambersburg PA
CBHW071502080526
44587CB00014B/2191